# Understanding American Schools

## The Answers to Newcomers' Most Frequently Asked Questions

### FOURTH EDITION

Anne P. Copeland, PhD
*The Interchange Institute*
and
Georgia Bennett
*Bennett Schoolplacement Worldwide*

A Publication of
The Interchange Institute

**The Interchange Institute**

11 Hawes Street

Brookline, MA 02446

telephone (617) 566-2227

www.interchangeinstitute.org

info@interchangeinstitute.org

Copyright © 2011. Anne P. Copeland and Georgia Bennett.

Earlier editions of this book have been catalogued as follows:

**Publisher's Cataloging-in-Publication**

Copeland, Anne P., 1951-
    Understanding American schools : the answers to newcomers' most frequently asked questions / Anne P. Copeland and Georgia Bennett.
    p. cm.
    Includes index.
    LCCN: 2002283813

    1. Education-United States.    I. Bennett, Georgia.
    II. Title.

LA210.C67 2005                371'.00973
                              QBI02-200557

The
Interchange
Institute

The Interchange Institute is a not-for-profit institution specializing in assisting families relocating globally. The Institute conducts research on the impact of intercultural transitions on individuals and families. From the results of this research, a variety of services are provided, including workshops and training, publications and products, and consulting services. For more information, visit www.interchangeinstitute.org.

www.schoolplacement.com
Since 1991

Bennett Schoolplacement Worldwide specializes in school and college placement services worldwide, educational consulting for relocating families, guides to schools in locations worldwide, and support for Human Resource professionals on all aspects of education policy planning. For more information, visit www.schoolplacement.com.

# Table of Contents

## CHAPTER 6: THE EARLY YEARS

## CHAPTER 7: DAILY CUSTOMS AND PRACTICAL ISSUES

## CHAPTER 8: ACADEMIC CURRICULUM

### CHAPTER 9: THE ROLE OF PARENTS, THE HOME, AND COMMUNITY

## CHAPTER 10: HIGH SCHOOL ISSUES

# Introduction

If you are a parent of a school-age child and are moving to the United States, the first thing you must do is make two closely-linked decisions:

- Where will your child go to school?
- Where will you live?

For reasons that we will discuss in the first chapter, schools in the U.S. are very varied — perhaps more varied than in any other developed country. Whether you are considering private or public schools, international schools or religion-based ones, you will find a wide range of educational quality, teaching methods, rules, available funding, and curriculum (although within any one school district, these factors will be similar). So when you begin to look for a home, be sure you evaluate the nearby schools at the same time.

In our work with international newcomers to the U.S. (as a psychologist and an educational consultant), we have come to know the many ways the American educational system surprises people from other countries. We wrote this book to help you sort out the sometimes confusing choices, rules, systems, and customs you may face when you start the process of choosing an American school. We have tried to answer the questions you might have about American schools, including the practical information you will need in order to select and get your child settled in an American school, as well as a description of the history and values behind the American system. Because the American education system is very de-centralized, it is difficult to make generalizations about some aspects of schooling. And because we have written this book for people from all over the world, specific comparisons to other countries' education systems could not be included. Still, there is much to say about the American education system that will be true no matter where you live.

There are two ways to use this book. We suggest that you read Chapter 1, no matter what your questions are. In this way, you'll learn more about why American schools are run as they are. Then, either start with Chapter 2 and read straight through — you'll probably learn the answers to some questions before you have even asked them! Or, for a faster solution to a specific problem, use the Table of Contents, the index at the end, and the headings to get just the answers to your immediate questions.

Use this book alongside the information you receive from the schools you are considering and/or the information you learn on the Internet. You will find a lot of information about specific schools — forms, requirements, calendars, rules, course information, and more — on the Internet. The National Center for Education Statistics lists quite a bit of information about each school and school district at nces.ed.gov/ccd. You can compare school districts on financial and demographic terms by going to nces.ed.gov/surveys/sdds/main1.asp. Or compare schools you are considering at these sites: www.schoolmatters.com or www.greatschools.net. Or ask a friend, co-worker, or relocation professional to help you find the web site addresses for your school district.

One last bit of advice: unless you decide to place your child in a school built on your home country's educational approach (and even then), do not look for a school that is "just like home." You will not find it. Private and public schools in the U.S. are uniquely American and will likely offer a different educational experience than you are used to. Look instead for a school that you think will benefit your child, one that offers a new approach, a new opportunity, a new context for learning.

Your child's enrollment in an American school may be your most important entrée into American culture. You will be side by side with American parents who share your educational hopes and concerns. You will encounter some cultural differences that will be part of your international experience. You will see and be a part of the most human side of American culture: families and communities working together to raise their children. You will be invited —indeed, expected — to become involved in the daily workings of the school. If you ever have questions or concerns, talk with the teachers or office staff — they are there to help with your child's transition to the American school system. Choose your school carefully, then stay involved. We hope this book helps you understand why and how to do both.

Anne P. Copeland
Georgia Bennett

# CHAPTER 1
## The American Educational Context

### THE LONG VIEW

- *A teacher tells a 12-year-old's mother that her child is "doing well" in school, but then the child does not get all A's on her report card.*

- *A child who will go on to become a university professor goes to the same school, and, depending on her age, is in some or all of the same classes as a student who will grow up to be a house painter.*

- *A second-grade teacher refuses to tell a parent how her child compares to other students in the class.*

- *A future doctor is required to study literature, psychology, history, philosophy, and math — in addition to science — until age 20 or 21.*

- *A first-grade teacher tells her children to write stories without worrying about proper spelling.*

- *An art teacher thinks too much technical drawing instruction might interfere with children's creativity.*

- *Math students get credit for using the right operations even if they get the answer wrong.*

In the United States these scenes happen every day, in the best schools. As you prepare to select and then place your child into an American school, you will want to understand why American educators do what they do. It will be helpful to understand something about the Long View that American educators take. Although this is not a book about university education, learning about American education after high (secondary) school will help you understand what happens in the American primary and secondary classroom. Remember, American teachers are preparing their students for life in the U.S., and in particular, for success in the American system, which tends to assume that students will receive well-rounded schooling until age 18 and often until age 22 or more. Educational decisions, from kindergarten through high school, are made in the context of the following four factors:

1. **A high proportion of American students enter and complete post-secondary education, and have done so for many decades** (see Chart). There are more than 4,000 colleges and universities in the U.S., many of which — not just one or two — are considered "top ranked." Any reasonably good student who wants a university education (and can afford it) can get one. This has several consequences for children in American schools. While many American parents put pressure on children to do well so they can be admitted to a good college or university, school-based competition, especially in the lower grades, is not as intense as in many other countries. At the same time, however, because so many students apply for university admission, factors other than exam scores and grades have become important as a way to stand out from the crowd, and as a sign that the student is emotionally stable and well-rounded. In addition to academic excellence, you will see teachers emphasizing sports, arts, music, and community involvement, as well as leadership and good social skills.

2. **Most university degree programs require the study of a wide range of topics other than the area of specialty.** All the way through high school, and continuing throughout the four years of college/university, most American students study the "liberal arts" regardless of their future specialty. (There are a few exceptions in cities that have specialized

## Percent of Population age 25-64 who Completed Tertiary Education

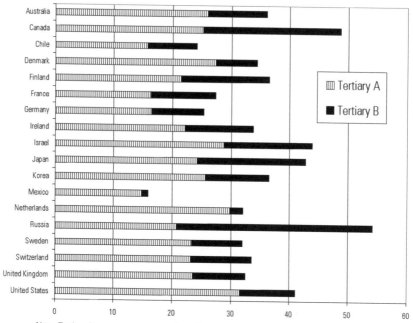

Note: Tertiary A programs prepare students for advanced degrees and/or high-skill professions; Tertiary B programs prepare them directly for the labor market. In recent years, many countries have seen a significant increase in the number of students starting tertiary education. This chart about 25-64-year-olds shows the effect of high-university enrollment in the U.S. over many years. It is this long-standing expectation of high university enrollment that has had an impact on primary and secondary education.

Source: Organization for Economic Co-operation and Development (OECD)

high schools for those interested in the sciences or performing arts.) The liberal arts include science, mathematics, foreign language, humanities, and social science. University students are typically not required to pick a specialty (called a
"major") until their second or third year — that is, about age
19 or 20 — and even then, they continue to take courses outside their major. Professional education (for doctors, lawyers,
academics, etc.) begins after this four-year liberal arts education. The philosophy is that everyone — business people,
doctors, and artists alike — should be well-trained in all of
these fields. Your high school student will, therefore, not
have to (in fact, will not be allowed to) study just a few sub-

## WORDS TO KNOW

**Freshman** – high school 9th grader or first-year college student

**Sophomore** – high school 10th grader or second-year college student

**Junior** – high school 11th grader or third-year college student

**Senior** – high school 12th grader or fourth-year college student

**College vs. University** – both terms usually refer to a 4-year post-secondary program leading to a bachelor's degree (although some offer a 2-year program leading to an associate's degree). Universities are not necessarily higher quality than colleges. Colleges are usually smaller than universities and may include only liberal arts education. Universities include more than one "school" or "college" or division (like a nursing school, a school of engineering, or a law school) in addition to a liberal arts division, and/or at least one graduate (post-bachelor's) program. The phrase "going to college" simply means going to one of these kinds of programs, not necessarily a college rather than a university.

**School** – refers to education at all levels, from preschool through doctoral and professional programs

**Undergraduate** – a student at a [post-secondary] college or university

**Grad Student** – short for "graduate student," that is, a student who has graduated from a college or university and is working toward a master's, doctoral, or professional degree (for example in medicine, law, or engineering)

---

jects. And American teachers in the lower grades, knowing that most of their students will study each subject again at a later age in more depth, may not insist on as full mastery of concepts as you might expect or like.

3. **There are lots of "second chances" in the American system.** Most American educators believe that children develop intellectually at different rates and that it is important to keep open the possibilities for "late bloomers" to succeed. Students are usually not put into classes based on their ability until middle school, or even later (although some elementary schools have programs for "gifted and talented children"). Students who

have done poorly in high school can still be admitted to an excellent college or university, by demonstrating emotional or intellectual growth at a community college or by working for a year or two before applying for university admission.

## Age at which Tracking and Specialization Occur in the U.S.

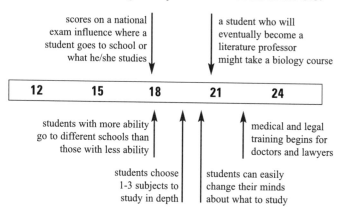

4. **To succeed in one's career in the U.S., it is neither necessary nor sufficient to have gone to one of the best universities.** While the "top universities and colleges" offer an excellent educational exposure to faculty and peers with similar skills and interest, a diploma from one of these schools does not guarantee a successful career or even an excellent first job. It is true that college graduates earn higher salaries (almost double, in fact) than those who only finished high school. But *which* college or university one goes to is less clearly related to life outcome. One study compared those who graduated from the most elite colleges with those who had been admitted to those same colleges but went elsewhere; 20 years later, their incomes were the same. Of the 100 U.S. Senators, 18 earned their undergraduate degrees from Ivy League (most elite) colleges. A recent report by *U.S. News*

*and World Report* stated that, of the top 10 Fortune 500 company CEOs, just three attended an Ivy League college. One can see a similar trend if you look at the resumes of the winners of Rhodes Scholarships. In short, one can succeed in American life without the best credentials. Therefore, while good high school students certainly feel pressure to do well, doing well in high school is not a promise of life-long career success.

These factors, coupled with deeply-held American values, have molded the educational system in the U.S. in profound ways.

### WHAT AMERICAN TEACHERS VALUE

You will see the impact of these factors in the ways teachers teach, in what they teach, and in what they value, from kindergarten through high school. Although not all teachers actually behave in ways that are consistent with these values, they generally share a set of common beliefs:

**Children should be well rounded**. American teachers think that "getting good grades" is only a part of being a good student. They also value being well rounded. This means doing extracurricular activities (non-academic activities, like sports, art or music), being a good friend, and being a happy and friendly person. A teacher who describes a child as "a great student" is not simply talking about her grades (which might not be the highest in every subject). She is also talking about the child's other skills. Universities like students to be well rounded too. A student with all A's but no extracurricular activities may have trouble being admitted to an excellent American university. A student with some lower grades who is active in student government, music, or social service may be admitted first.

**Problem solving and creative thinking should be prized alongside skill development.** This value is clearest in American art classes, where "expressing yourself" is sometimes more important than learning to draw something realistic-looking. But it is present in other classes too. A teacher may urge a first-grade child to write long and complex stories, even if she cannot spell most of the words. The teacher's belief is that if children are expected to write stories using only the words they can spell correctly, the stories will be boring — to others and to the child. It is more important to keep the children interested in telling their ideas than to spell correctly (at least in the early grades). And in math and science, American teachers value learning to think conceptually about a problem — to think intuitively, to understand the process, to make hypotheses. "Rote memorization" of facts is recommended only for important basics, like multiplication tables and historical dates.

**Teachers should be creative, too.** Because of a relative lack of national, or even state-wide lesson plans, individual teachers are free, within a certain framework set by the school district, to develop their own ways of teaching. Of course there are guidelines and helpful teaching materials available to them. But it is common to find one teacher teaching about butterflies by making plaster models of a chrysalis while the teacher next door is plugging her children onto the Internet to track the migration of the monarch butterfly. Perhaps more than in your country, the American system is open to a range in quality of teaching, reflected in teachers' varying experience, creativity, and available resources.

**Individualism is good and should be taught.** American teachers encourage every child to be unique, and they highly value any sign that a child thinks for him or herself. You will see teachers of very young children offering choices that may surprise you: "Do you want a red pencil or a blue one?" "Do you want to do math first or spelling?" And even, "What book do you want to read now?" Your children will be encouraged to speak their opinions aloud, to challenge or respectfully disagree with the teacher's opinions, and to speak in front of the group about their ideas and activities. These are all ways that individualism is taught. The teachers, in turn, individualize their students' work. Although children of all ability levels may be in a single classroom, they may be doing very different work — different kinds of math problems, reading different books, learning to spell different words — all to match their abilities.

**% Time Teachers Spend with Individual Students or Small Groups**

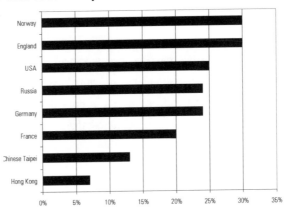

*Source: Progress in International Reading Literacy Stidu*

**Informality and minimal social hierarchies are good.** You may hear American children calling their teachers by their first names. They may complain to their teachers about assignments. They may argue with their teachers — about a rule, or about a concept being taught. This may sound like disrespect to you. But

## How Are Educational Values Put into Practice?

How are these values put into practice? Here is a list of teaching methods that some American experts* consider good and bad.

In a "**bad**" school (say the American experts), you will see:
- a lot of direct instruction by the teacher,
- students spending a lot of time listening quietly and receiving information,
- a lot of practice worksheets and workbooks, in which one concept is practiced repeatedly,
- a lot of time spent reading textbooks,
- much effort to teach many different topics (if that means you cannot teach them in depth),
- an emphasis on rote memorization and testing of memorized facts,
- competition for good grades, and
- many tests.

In contrast, in a "**good**" school, you will see:
- students experimenting with ideas to see which ones are true,
- students doing and talking,
- more study of a few topics in depth,
- students reading whole books, written as literature or history, not textbooks,
- students deciding for themselves how good their work is,
- students themselves choosing what to learn,
- a focus on the emotional needs of the students,
- teachers writing summaries and descriptions of the students rather than giving test scores.

Do you agree with the classification as "bad" and "good" here?

\* *Zemelman, Daniels, and Hyde, Best Practices: New Standards for Teaching and Learning in America's Schools (Heinemann, 1993)*

it is useful to see this behavior as a reflection of Americans' belief that everyone should be treated equally. Of course, Americans do not always treat everyone equally. But American teachers tend to believe that a system that does not emphasize social hierarchy is better for learning. Some allow children to use their first names. They encourage the children to make their own choices about what they will study, and how they will study it. They consider arguing — at least about concepts — to be proof that the child is actively involved in the learning. They may even consider children's complaints to be a good sign that they are learning to express their opinions clearly.

You have come to the U.S. at a time of great public discussion about these values and how they influence the quality of schools. Americans are asking, "How can we improve science and math education?" "Whose job is it — schools' or families' — to teach respect and ethics?" "Have we overdone our emphasis on problem-solving and creativity at the expense of mastery of basic skills?" "What are parents entitled to do if their local schools are not good enough?" "What should be the role of the federal government in ensuring all children get a good education?"

American educators are studying the classroom approaches in countries with high-scoring students and considering how to adapt these approaches into the U.S. system. As you learn more about what American educators are trying to accomplish, you can add your voice and values to this discussion.

### WHO MAKES THE DECISIONS ABOUT SCHOOLS IN THE U.S.?

You may be surprised to learn that most decisions about education in the U.S. are made by the states and local districts, not the federal (national) government (although the federal government has been increasing its role in recent years - see the Chart on the next page for details). This is consistent with a deeply-held American belief — rooted in the 18th century American Revolution and written into the U.S. Constitution — that decisions should be made at a level as close to the  people as possible. You will notice many state-to-state differences, like in speed limits, election procedures, rules about buying alcohol, and, importantly, education.

# Percent of Educational Decisions Made at Different Levels

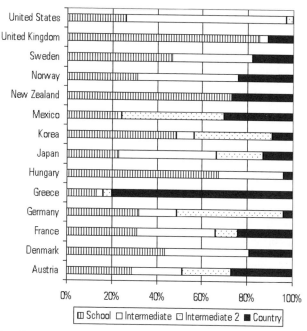

☐ School ☐ Intermediate ☐ Intermediate 2 ■ Country

Note: This chart shows where four types of educational decisions (planning and structure, personnel management, organization of instruction, and resources) are made. The "Intermediate" level is the one closest to the school — in the case of the U.S., this refers to the school district. "Intermediate 2" refers to the regional level — the state in the U.S. system. Higher levels may still influence decision-making by consulting with schools and/or by setting legal or regulatory frameworks that the schools and districts must obey. This certainly happens in the U.S., as states influence school districts' decisions in these ways.

Source: Organization for Economic Co-operation and Development (OECD)

States differ from each other in how they share educational decision-making with school districts, but, in one way or another, they, not the federal government, decide what subjects to teach, what teaching methods to approve, when a child may graduate from high school, what kind of special education to offer, which books to use, how to judge the progress of each child's education, how many days and hours of school to require, and the like.

The U.S. federal government's influence on education has traditionally been indirect, through two channels. First, federal officials can use their status to try to *persuade* schools to change policies. The weight of national recommendations may persuade some states' educators to adopt teaching and curricular guidelines. Even so, the most recent effort at establishing national curriculum norms, The Common Core State Standards Initiative, came from the national [state] governors' association and a group of non-government education experts, not the federal government. (See these standards at www.corestandards.org.)

Second, the federal government influences education through its *funding* priorities. If the federal government gives research money to study drug education or parental choice of schools, these programs become more common. It gives money to schools for specific programs

## Where Are Educational Decisions Made?

| | national | state | school district | principal | teacher | student | | national | state | school district | principal | teacher | student |
|---|---|---|---|---|---|---|---|---|---|---|---|---|---|
| 1. number of hours in the school day | □ | □ | □ | □ | □ | □ | | □ | □ | √ | □ | □ | □ |
| 2. number of days in the school year | □ | □ | □ | □ | □ | □ | | □ | √ | □ | □ | □ | □ |
| 3. how much teachers are paid | □ | □ | □ | □ | □ | □ | | □ | □ | √ | √ | □ | □ |
| 4. at what age children will learn about ancient Egypt | □ | □ | □ | □ | □ | □ | | □ | □ | √ | □ | □ | □ |
| 5. what children will eat for lunch | □ | □ | □ | □ | □ | □ | | □ | □ | √ | □ | □ | √ |
| 6. how many field trips a class will take | □ | □ | □ | □ | □ | □ | | □ | □ | √ | √ | √ | □ |
| 7. starting date of school in the fall | □ | □ | □ | □ | □ | □ | | □ | □ | √ | □ | □ | □ |
| 8. what students must know to graduate | □ | □ | □ | □ | □ | □ | | □ | √ | √ | □ | √ | □ |
| 9. which books will be used | □ | □ | □ | □ | □ | □ | | □ | √ | √ | √ | √ | √ |
| 10. at what age children must go to school | □ | □ | □ | □ | □ | □ | | □ | √ | □ | □ | □ | □ |
| 11. teacher qualifications to be hired | □ | □ | □ | □ | □ | □ | | □ | √ | √ | □ | □ | □ |
| 12. whether schools will close because of snow | □ | □ | □ | □ | □ | □ | | □ | □ | √ | □ | □ | □ |
| 13. whether there will be after-school sports programs | □ | □ | □ | □ | □ | □ | | □ | □ | √ | √ | □ | □ |
| 14. how much time a child should spend on homework each night | □ | □ | □ | □ | □ | □ | | □ | □ | □ | □ | √ | □ |
| 15. whether children will be taught physical education | □ | □ | □ | □ | □ | □ | | □ | □ | √ | □ | □ | □ |
| 16. which foreign language to study | □ | □ | □ | □ | □ | □ | | □ | □ | √ | □ | □ | √ |
| 17. ensuring that minority children are not discriminated against | □ | □ | □ | □ | □ | □ | | √ | √ | √ | √ | √ | √ |
| TOTAL | _ | _ | _ | _ | _ | _ | | 1 | 6 | 14 | 5 | 5 | 4 |

*In the left-hand set of boxes, consider where educational decisions are made in your country. In the right-hand set of boxes is a summary of where they are typically made in the U.S.*

## INCREASING FEDERAL ROLE IN EDUCATION

The federal *No Child Left Behind Act* of 2002 (NCLB) was established as an accountability system for states, school districts, and schools receiving federal education funds. It requires states and local districts to (1) have academic standards, (2) make annual progress toward having every student achieve the standards, (3) test students to see if they are learning, and (4) collect data on how they are doing. The law also requires states to identify schools and school districts that are not making enough progress and to follow a step-by-step process for either turning those schools around or closing them.

The NCLB Act has been highly debated. Critics feel it is too punitive in nature and is unrealistic, given the varied make-up of individual schools. It has also been criticized for its lack of funding and its test-focused approach. To comply with the Act, many schools turned their attention and resources almost exclusively to math and reading, leaving the arts and enrichment opportunities with little to no funding.

In recent years, a second federal education initiative, *Race to the Top* (RTTT), was introduced. RTTT allowed states to compete for federal funding for K-12 education, rather than automatically receive it. As part of this "federal stimulus" act, Congress provided $4.35 billion for competitive grants to states to encourage education innovation and reform in four areas: (1) enhancing standards and assessments, (2) improving collection and use of data, (3) increasing teacher effectiveness and achieving equity in teacher distribution, and (4) turning around low-achieving schools. Winning states were required to use the grant money to implement the programs and plans detailed in their grant applications.

What's next? The federal government continues to address educational reform. And educators and politicians continue to debate testing as a way to measure the performance of schools, teachers and students - how flexible should the measurement schemes be to respond to local conditions, and what should be measured (e.g. individual student scores, graduation rates, performance in a variety of subjects, school performance over time)? A balance between federal demand for accountability and local demand for flexibility will surely continue to be sought, in education as in other aspects of American life.

believed to be in the national interest, like:

- school lunches for children from low-income families,
- programs in science, math, and foreign language,
- reading help for children who are "educationally deprived,"
- job training.

Then, to enforce values it sees as basic to all Americans, the federal government will stop sending this money to school districts that discriminate against any group of children. This has been important in improving the education of minority children, non-English-speaking children, and children with disabilities.

Finally, the federal government has offered money to states that adhere to standards outlined in its *No Child Left Behind Act* and the *Race to the Top* initiative (see Box). These programs have increased the role of the federal government in educational decisions, and are currently being debated in light of states' experience in conforming with their demands. There will likely be a continuing federal emphasis on the measurement of performance by schools, teachers and students; flexible but meaningful evaluation methods for schools; and a concern with a range of subjects and educational goals.

**ALL SCHOOLS ARE NOT CREATED EQUAL**

Both public and private schools across the U.S., and even within a state, differ in the quality of their teachers, class size, facilities, and the achievement of their students, for a number of reasons:

**Public School Funding and Quality.** Across the U.S., most public school funding is roughly split between the state and local governments (see Chart on the next page). States and local districts differ widely in the tax rates they approve and in their budget choices. Therefore, some school districts have more money to spend than others. Public schools within a district, however, tend to be similar in quality and funding.

In comparing public schools and school districts, one factor to consider is the school district's level of spending per student. Ask your school district office for these figures. Study the school district "profile" for the "per student" expenditure amount. The National Center for Education Statistics posts these numbers on their website: nces.ed.gov/ccd/schoolsearch (search for your school district). These profiles are also printed in many different publications and are available by asking at the school or any public library. Comparing per-student spending level with the national level ($10,600) will probably be meaningless, since the cost of living varies so much from state to state. But you may find a comparison of spending in the several districts you are considering to be useful (try nces.ed.gov/surveys/sdds/main1.asp).

You will also probably see a comparison of district test scores and other measures of educational quality. See Chapter 4 for a discussion of what these comparison measures do, and do not, mean. In general, do not use any single statistic as your only measure of quality.

### Source of Public School Funds

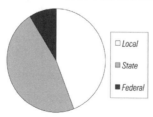

☐ Local

▨ State

■ Federal

This chart shows the U.S. national average for source of funds. States differ considerably — in Vermont, for example, 5.6% of funds come from local sources, 86.9% from the state; in Nevada, 65.4 come from local sources, 27.1% from the state.

*Source: National Education Association*

**Private School Funding and Quality.** Private schools' operating budgets are made up primarily of tuition income, charitable donations, endowment income, and, in some cases, funds from sponsoring organizations (like religious groups). Parents who choose private education for their children often make a substantial economic sacrifice to do so. They believe that the investment is necessary to ensure that their children are in a supportive environment with qualified teachers and a curriculum that embodies their values and standards — whether religious, philosophical, academic or social.

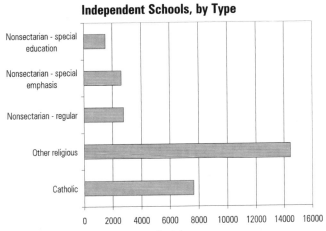

### Independent Schools, by Type

*Source: National Center for Education Statistics*

It is important to remember that there is also a range in quality of private schools. Private schools may offer smaller class sizes and better facilities than many (but not all) public schools. In addition, private schools may have a reputation for offering some specific approach to education. For example, one may be known as a school that emphasizes academic basics. Another may be known for its integrated, creative learning, and another for its focus on student-directed learning. Some schools may be very strict, and others very lenient. Schools run by religious organizations usually include some religious instruction. If you are considering a private school, do not simply take a friend's recommendation that it is a "good school" — the friend's preferred educational philosophy may be very different from yours.

**Accreditation of Schools.** Both public school systems and private schools (which include independent schools and religion-based schools) must comply with all state guidelines for graduation and enrollment requirements. Private schools often have even more requirements than the states. In addition, both private and public schools must comply with the guidelines of their accrediting body. To be accredited, a school goes through a rigorous process administered by other school officials selected for their expertise. Strong private schools should either be accredited by one of the organizations shown in the Box below, or in the process of seeking accreditation.

---

SOME HIGHLY-RESPECTED SCHOOL ACCREDITING BOARDS
- Association of Christian Schools International
- European Council of International Schools
- International Baccalaureate North America
- International Baccalaureate Organization
- Middle States Association of Colleges and Schools
- National Association of Independent Schools
- New England Association of Colleges and Schools
- North Central Association of Colleges and Schools
- Southern Association of Colleges and Schools

---

**Urban vs. Suburban Schools.** Urban schools face a particular challenge in that they must educate large numbers of children from a wide variety of cultural, financial, and linguistic backgrounds. The challenge is often made more difficult by the fact that many urban families with the financial means to do so choose to send their children to independent or religion-based schools, causing the public schools to lose educated, financially secure and influential parents — the very people whose involvement is critical to the maintenance and improvement of the schools' standards.

The urban public school systems have some advantages, however. Many have a more international student body and, therefore, bigger bilingual or English as a Second Language programs. [These programs may be referred to as ESL, ELL (English Language Learning), EAL (English as an Additional Language), or something comparable.] In addition, these systems are often large enough to support special schools not found elsewhere. Generally more academic, these special schools frequently center around a particular field or subject. For example, there may be a high school of International Affairs, of Science, or of the Creative and Performing Arts. With some exceptions, students must apply to these schools despite their being public, and if admitted, may attend as long as they live within the city limits.

Suburban school districts, compared to their urban and rural counterparts, tend to be better funded and have a higher percentages of university-bound students. Neither of those advantages, however, necessarily translates into a better education environment.

**Summary**: In short, overall quality of schools varies tremendously, and there is no single indicator that reliably distinguishes the stronger programs from the weaker. The information in the following chapters will help you understand the different factors and statistics you may see as you begin to compare schools.

# CHAPTER 2
## Choosing the Type of School Your Child Will Attend

### WHAT CHOICES DO WE HAVE?

Most American children go to *public* schools, that is, schools that are paid for by government taxes and are open and free to residents of the community. About 11% attend *private* schools. Among more affluent segments of the population, particularly in very urban areas, the percentage going to private schools may be 50% or higher. Private schools come in a wide range of types. In addition to independent schools that emphasize a general, non-

---

**WORDS TO KNOW**

**private school:** a school to which students must pay a tuition fee to attend; this term includes both independent and religion-based schools

**religion-based school:** a private school that is sponsored by a religious organization; the curriculum usually includes some religious instruction and services; some common sponsoring organizations are Christian, Catholic, Episcopal, Jewish, and Quaker ("Friends")

**parochial school:** a religion-based school run by a local Catholic diocese; many of these schools are attached to a Catholic church

**independent school:** a private, non-religion-based school

**magnet school:** public schools with a specialized teaching approach or specialization in one subject area (like science, the arts, or bilingual education); these often attract students from anywhere in the district (not just the immediate neighborhood)

**charter school:** a public school funded by the public school system but independent of it in many ways; these are usually set up by a group of parents or teachers who feel they can offer a better or different educational experience by being free of the control of the public school system

**vouchers:** government-provided funds that families can use to help pay tuition costs at a private school

---

sectarian education, you may find religion-based schools, schools for children with specific types of learning disabilities, schools with a therapy component in addition to the academic program, boarding schools, sports academies, fine arts or music schools, schools for orphans, military schools, Montessori schools, international schools, and national curriculum schools, and many others.

In recent years, some communities have allowed parents to choose from among their public schools. Others have set up *magnet schools* for children with special interests, needs or preferences. Others have allowed public school funds to be used to run *charter schools*, which are somewhat independent of the school district's oversight. Still others give *vouchers*, or funds that parents can use to help pay for private schools. These programs (described in more detail later in this chapter) are controversial, as critics worry that they will weaken the public school system. Supporters of the programs claim that the competition they provoke is good for the public school system and has led to improvements in it. Ask if such choice is available in the communities you are considering.

### WHICH PUBLIC SCHOOL WILL MY CHILD ATTEND?

Generally, a public school must admit any child living in its district, even if the child has special learning problems or does not speak English. (Check the rules that apply to your visa status, however; students on F-1 visas may not be able to attend public high schools for free, although students on F-2 visas can.)

Some districts offer parents some choice of schools within the district. In other communities, the location of a home determines which school a child will attend. Many relocating parents choose

## Where Children Go to School, Grades 1-12

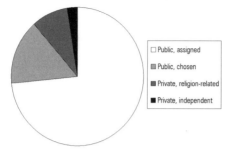

- ☐ Public, assigned
- ▦ Public, chosen
- ■ Private, religion-related
- ■ Private, independent

*Source: The Condition of Education; US Department of Education*

a few good schools or school districts and then look for homes within those catchment areas (the zones served by particular schools). In some rare cases, a district may decide that a school (or a grade within that school) is full. In that case, children who otherwise would go to that school must go to a different school within the district; the district will provide bus transportation for those children if the distance is great. It is always a good idea, therefore, to ask if you have any choice, and to confirm ahead of time that, if you live in a certain district, your child will be guaranteed a place at a specific school.

Township and school-district boundaries are not always the same. The most reliable source of information about which public school serves your neighborhood is the local school district office. They will be able to tell you your catchment area and the school your children will attend. The most reliable place to find school district telephone numbers is on a school or district's website (easily found using an internet search engine such as Google or Yahoo). You may also find their numbers in the government section (often the "blue pages") of the local telephone directory.

In some cases, your children may be allowed to go to a school outside your catchment area in order to attend a program that meets their special language or learning needs, or that simply is preferable to you. In other cases, you may have the option of sending your child to a public school in a different district for a fee, provided the preferred school has space and is willing to make the exception. These rules vary from district to district.

### How much does it cost to go to a public school?

Public schools are "free" to you (and remember that you will be paying for them indirectly through taxes and/or rent whether or not your children go there). Parents may be asked to pay occasionally for special activities such as field trips or sports equipment, but payment is never required for families who do not have the money. In general, public schools make an effort to make all educational opportunities available to all eligible students regardless of the family's financial situation. Some schools have free or reduced-fee meals for children who cannot afford to pay. If your child is asked to bring money to school that you do not have, talk to someone in the school office or your child's teacher.

### Who can go to a private school?

Students must apply directly to private schools and undergo their admissions procedures. Some schools have highly competitive admissions standards. Applying to more than one is entirely acceptable and usually recommended. Private schools often require special tests, interviews, and letters of recommendation (from past teachers, family friends, or community leaders who know the child). Some private schools are highly selective and conduct their admissions according to a strict schedule. For example, an application deadline may be in January for a September start, and interviews may have to be scheduled far in advance. Plan ahead as much as possible.

There are no catchment areas for private schools, with the exception of certain parochial schools run by a local Catholic archdiocese. Students need only to live close enough to commute easily. However, you may want to ask about where other students in the school live. Living near other students will help your child make friends and participate in social activities outside of school.

### HOW MUCH DOES IT COST TO GO TO A PRIVATE SCHOOL?

Private schools charge a tuition fee, which varies greatly depending on the age of the student, the type of school, and the part of the U.S. in which the school is located. Parochial schools tend to be less expensive: an average of $10,000 per year at the secondary level. Tuition for private day schools ranges from about $16,000 to $30,000, and can be even higher in urban areas. In New York City, for example, secondary private school tuition is usually about $35,000. At boarding schools, the total bill often exceeds $45,000 because of the additional costs of housing and meals. Schools with therapy components may be more than twice as expensive as standard schools. (Private-school costs tend to rise by approximately 8% per year.)

When asking about private school costs, always ask for the tuition figures and all other required and "optional fees." Optional fees may include costs like school bus transportation that you may want to consider.

Private schools also depend on donations of money from individuals to help meet operating costs. If your child is enrolled in a private school, expect to be asked to make additional contributions in addition to the tuition and fees. These contributions are voluntary but be aware that the fund raisers, often other parents and graduates, may be quite direct and persistent in their efforts.

Some financial aid and scholarship money is usually available from private schools. Almost all of it is granted on the basis of financial need. Ask the admissions officer at the school about what financial help, if any, the school itself can provide and what other grants and scholarships might be available. You should not feel reluctant or shy about asking about financial aid. Schools expect you to ask about it and, if they have financial aid budgets, are eager to identify worthy recipients of that aid. Your inquiries will be considered confidential within the admissions department.

### WHAT ARE "BOARDING SCHOOLS?"

Boarding schools are private schools where students live full-time, although many boarding schools also accept day students. Boarding schools often draw students from across the country and abroad. Some offer the opportunity to be part of an educational environment with an international flavor even though they are located in a suburban or rural area. Boarding schools come in a wide range of types. A number are very academic and college directed. Some focus on outdoor education and environmental sciences. Others combine academic and therapeutic programs. There are boarding schools with large international populations. All generally offer supportive learning environments, relatively small class sizes, accessible faculty and extensive facilities. Boarding schools can offer an excellent alternative for families relocating for only a short period of time, or to an area where the local school alternatives don't adequately meet the student's needs. Some children are eager to be "on their own" before they reach university/college age and some benefit from the structured, supportive and demanding learning environments that boarding schools are particularly good at providing.

## WHAT IS AN "INTERNATIONAL SCHOOL?"

The term "international school" is sometimes used loosely in the U.S. Technically, an international school is one that offers a curriculum and/or finishing certificate based on some other educational system in addition to the American one. Many international schools offer more than one finishing certificate: the American high school diploma, some other national curriculum program diploma, and/or the International Baccalaureate, for example. In some cases, students may fulfill the requirements of, and be awarded, more than one finishing certificate. The curricula and programs of international schools are structured to meet the needs of students from varied educational backgrounds.

Schools fitting this description don't always refer to themselves as "international" and they may be public, private, church-affiliated, boarding or day. To make matters more confusing, some schools that call themselves "international" have a virtually all-American curriculum, faculty and student body. As with all schools, the name and the affiliation are less important than the quality and types of programs provided. Be sure to research these programs as you consider your choices. (Also, see *The Guide to International Education in the United States* described in the Box below.)

---

### THE GUIDE TO INTERNATIONAL EDUCATION IN THE UNITED STATES

*The Guide to International Education in the United States: National Curriculum and International Schools*, a publication of Bennett Schoolplacement Worldwide (formerly Bennett Educational Resources, Inc.), lists international and IB schools, and British, French, German, Italian, Japanese, and Spanish national curriculum schools in the U.S. It includes schools' nationality and location, names of directors, grade levels and school day format, date established and current enrollment numbers, and accreditation granting organization. First edition, 2005. Order at www.schoolplacement.com.

---

## WHAT IS A "MAGNET SCHOOL?"

Some school districts, especially urban ones, have magnet schools, so-called because they attract students from anywhere in the district (not just the immediate neighborhood) with a specialized teaching approach (like "open education" or "back to basics" systems) or specialization in one subject area (like science, the arts, or bilingual education). Some magnet schools require students to apply for admission, and are selective because of limited space. There are over 3000 magnet schools (most of them elementary schools) in the U.S., with enrollments of 2.3 million students.

## WHAT IS A "CHARTER SCHOOL?"

A charter school is a public school that is funded by local and state government, but allowed to operate free of many bureaucratic regulations that apply to traditional public school districts. Charter school founders are often teachers, parents, or activists who feel restricted by traditional public schools and seek to offer students and their families more innovation and choice. In exchange for more autonomy, the school is bound to the terms of a contract or "charter" granted by state education authorities that lays out the school's mission, academic goals, and accountability procedures.

Charter schools frequently emphasize particular fields of study (e.g., the Arts or Technology), or serve special populations of students (e.g., special education or at-risk students). One of the more popular charter school models is the "cyber" school, which entirely does away with the actual school buildings by delivering curriculum content via the Internet.

While performance results have been mixed, the concept of the charter school has been widely embraced in the U.S. Most charter schools use a lottery system to determine randomly which students are accepted. Many also have waiting lists. Since the first charter school opened in Minnesota in 1992, the charter school movement has grown to about 5000 schools operating nationwide, serving about 1.5 million students.

## WHAT ARE "VOUCHERS?"

School vouchers are government-provided funds that families can use to help pay tuition costs at a private school. Vouchers are designed to give families more choices for their children and to encourage public schools to improve in order to compete with the private ones. Critics argue that they divert funds and attention away from public schools. Voucher programs, though not new, are controversial and are available in only a few states and Washington D.C. Parents interested in private school for their children should not rely on voucher funding to cover the cost of tuition.

## CAN MY CHILD EARN AN INTERNATIONAL BACCALAUREATE DEGREE?

The International Baccalaureate (IB) Organization's program is offered at some primary, middle and high schools across the U.S. Go to www.ibo.org for a list of schools in your state (or call the U.S. regional office in Bethesda, Maryland, at 301-202-3000, with questions). The IB program was designed for students who move around the world. It offers a rigorous and challenging common curriculum, set of standards, and university entry credentials for students from many different countries.

About 90% of IB programs in the U.S. are in public schools (in contrast to other countries, where they tend to be in private schools). In some major U.S. cities, the IB is offered in magnet schools, available only to students living in the city school district. Some suburban public schools may offer the IB but a student may only qualify after taking rigorous testing to be admitted. Private schools may offer the IB as a way of attracting a gifted student group; here, too, there will be many prerequisites that are quite stringent. In total, about 750 U.S. high schools offer the IB Diploma program.

## CAN I SEND MY CHILD TO A SCHOOL BASED ON MY HOME COUNTRY'S CURRICULUM?

Across the U.S. there are national curriculum schools providing an officially sanctioned program in the home country language. There are national curriculum schools for French, German, Italian, Japanese and British families in selected areas across the country. The largest concentration of these schools can be found in the New York and Washington, DC areas. See the Box on earlier in this chapter for information about *The Guide to International Education* which lists these schools in the U.S.

## CAN MY CHILDREN GO TO A SCHOOL RUN BY A RELIGIOUS ORGANIZATION IF THAT IS NOT OUR RELIGION?

In most cases, yes. You may decide that the school in your community that best matches your values and educational goals is one that is run by a religious group even if you are not, yourself, a member of that religion. Your children will probably be expected to receive some religious instruction and/or participate in some religious services, and you will have to decide if that is acceptable to you. Some international families have reported that they have felt pressure from the school to join the religious group that sponsors the school. Others report no such pressure. Ask the school what the expectations for you and your children will be.

## SHOULD WE BE CONSIDERING SINGLE-SEX EDUCATION?

Evidence suggests that single-sex education may have substantial advantages, particularly for girls, at all levels. The benefits for both boys and girls include freedom from the distraction of the opposite sex (although this is also found on the "disadvantages" list for some students). Boys sometimes find the pace and temperament of an all-boys school to be a better match for them. And girls sometimes find they can be more involved in classroom discussions and leadership if they do not have to compete with boys.

CHAPTER 3
# School Structure

## AT WHAT AGE DO CHILDREN GO TO SCHOOL IN THE U.S.?

Each state makes its own law about when children must go to school. Most states require school attendance starting at age 6 or 7 (although a few states require attendance at age 5 or 8), continuing to age 16, 17, or 18. Most school districts also offer an optional year of kindergarten for no fee, one year before the required starting year; most American children go to kindergarten. Each school district makes its own rules about the birth date cut-off for enrollment into kindergarten. For example, in some districts, a child must have turned five years old by September 1 to enter kindergarten; in other districts, the cut-off birth date is different.

An increasing number of districts are now offering preschool programs for four-year-olds. Although they are typically not free of charge, they tend to be less expensive than private preschool options, and they do fill up quickly.

The first opportunity to earn a secondary school certificate (or high school diploma) is at the completion of 12th grade in high school, usually at age 17 or 18. About 86% of the U.S. population age 18 and older have completed high school.

## WHAT AGE CHILD WILL BE AT MY CHILD'S SCHOOL?

School districts differ in how they group children by age. Some common structures are shown in the Box on the next page. Typically, children go to elementary (sometimes called primary) school, which starts at kindergarten and ends with 5th or 6th grade. Then they may go to a middle school (sometimes called a

## Some Common Public School System Structures

| Grade | School Structure | | | Age | Curriculum |
|---|---|---|---|---|---|
| 12 | Senior High School | Senior High School | Senior High School | 17 | continue academic preparation; business and technical courses |
| 11 | | | | 16 | |
| 10 | | | | 15 | |
| 9 | Junior High School | | | 14 | students may have some choices; begin foreign languages; begin academic specialization or tracking |
| 8 | | Middle School | Elementary (Primary) School | 13 | |
| 7 | | | | 12 | |
| 6 | Elementary (Primary) School | | | 11 | |
| 5 | | Elementary (Primary) School | | 10 | reading, math, science, social studies, music, art, all subjects required for all students |
| 4 | | | | 9 | |
| 3 | | | | 8 | |
| 2 | | | | 7 | |
| 1 | | | | 6 | |
| K | | | | 5 | pre-academics, socialization |
| PS | Pre-School | | | 3-4 | social skills and play |

junior high school): 6th or 7th grade through 8th or 9th. Then senior high school (sometimes called upper school): 9th or 10th through 12th grades. Other schools and districts divide the years differently.

### HOW ARE CLASSES FORMED?

In most American elementary schools, children are placed into a class with 18-25 other children and one teacher (and sometimes a teacher's aide or student teacher). (The student-teacher ratio has been decreasing over time in the U.S., reflecting an educational philosophy that values individual attention — see Chart on next page.) The classroom teacher will teach the major academic subjects to that group of children for one academic year. The next year, a new grouping of children will be made and a new teacher assigned. (Occasionally a teacher will keep the same group of children for two years; keeping the same group for more than two years is rare.) The school may have specialty teachers to teach art, music, computers, and physical education.

Sometimes these specialty teachers work part-time in several different schools in the district.

The school tries to form diverse groups of children for each class, blending boys and girls, new and old friends, and children with different learning abilities and behavior styles. Because of the emphasis on individualized education within each classroom, these diverse groups work well. Although this is a complicated matching process, schools may welcome your input into what kind of environment you think will work best for your child.

In middle school and high school, children usually move from class to class to study each subject with a different teacher, a specialist in that topic. They will receive an individual schedule that tells them when, where, and with whom they will study math, science, etc. Some of these classes (especially the major acade-

**Student-Teacher Ratio in the U.S.**

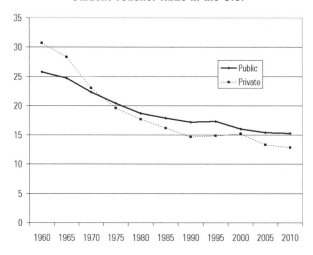

Note: This ratio includes all teaching staff, including specialists. Class size will be somewhat larger.

Source: National Center for Education Statistics

## Student-Teacher Ratio in Selected Countries

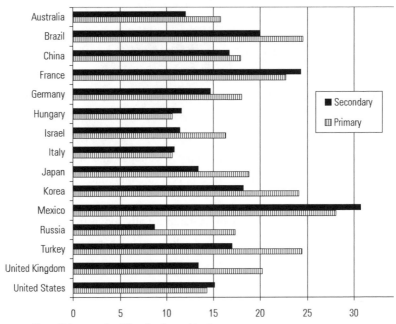

Note: Private and public schools combined

Source: Organization for Economic Co-operation and Development (OECD)

mic ones) may be formed on the basis of the children's ability level. If so, you and your children may have input into the levels to which they are assigned.

The size of each of your child's classes may vary significantly, depending on the subject being studied. While a ninth-grade English class might have as many as 30 students in it, for example, an advanced French Literature class might have many fewer students. Because of budget cuts in many school districts in recent years, it is a good idea to ask school personnel about the average class size in a school you are considering and what the immediate term plans are for reducing or increasing that number.

## ARE ACADEMICALLY-ORIENTED STUDENTS EDUCATED DIFFERENTLY THAN THOSE WHO WILL NOT GO ON TO UNIVERSITY?

In most public elementary and middle schools, all children are educated in the same schools, regardless of their abilities. However, American teachers begin individualizing children's learning from kindergarten on, so that children who excel in reading or math, for example, may get more challenging assignments than other students. Some schools begin to "track" (put children of different ability levels in different classes) in middle school.

In some communities or regions, there are vocational school alternatives to high schools, in which students learn job-related skills (like auto mechanics and food preparation) in addition to basic academics. But the majority of Americans go to a regular high school regardless of their academic future. Although there is some tracking based on ability in many high schools, American students who will go on to be university professors, doctors, and lawyers typically go to the same high schools (and may be in some of the same classes) as those who will not go on to higher education at all.

## WHO MAKES THE LOCAL DECISIONS ABOUT EDUCATION IN THE PUBLIC SCHOOLS?

As noted in Chapter 1, educational decisions in the U.S. are made largely at the local and state levels (although with increasing input by the federal government since the passage of the *No Child Left Behind Act*). Each state has a *Board* or *Department of Education* that makes some rules. Public school districts make most of the rest of the decisions. School districts are usually led by a group of 3-14 citizens who are elected and are not paid. These groups are called *school boards, school committees,* or *boards of education.* They make rules about budgets, teacher hiring, transportation, curriculum, and school buildings. A school *superintendent* (usually a paid professional) carries out the policies of this elected group.

Each public school building also has a *principal* whose job is to carry out the town's policies at that school. The principal oversees the building itself, the school's budget, teachers' schedules, and the assignment of children to teachers. In addition, the principal is important in setting the level of warmth and control in each school.

## FINDING INFORMATION ABOUT SCHOOLS

*Here are some ways to get detailed information about your community's public school system:*

- Look on the Internet:

  - The National Center for Education Statistics lists information about each school and school district at nces.ed.gov. You can compare school districts on financial and demographic terms by going to this site : nces.ed.gov/surveys/sdds/main1.asp.

  - Each state has a web site (www.state.___.us; insert your state's two-letter abbreviation instead of the "___") that will include some education information. Many communities, cities, and towns now also post comparative educational statistics. Because every state and community designs its own web site, however, educational information may be a challenge to find.

  - Try www.schoolmatters.com or www.greatschools.net for comparative information.

- Call your state Department of Education. Many have some kind of Parent Information Center that will send you complete data about a town's school size, money spent per student, performance in reading, math, science, social studies, and writing, college-entrance exam scores, teacher salaries, etc.

- Talk with an educational consultant who knows your community and your needs.

- Ask your public librarian to help you find information.

*For information about private schools:*

- Ask the Admissions Office of a particular school to mail you information, or ask if the school has a web site.

- Read a brief summary in one of the many guides to private schools that exist (like *Peterson's Private Secondary Schools)* which your U.S. public library will probably have, or go to www.petersons.com/private.

- Talk with an educational consultant who knows your community and your needs.

CHAPTER 4
## Comparing Schools

**HOW CAN I LEARN ABOUT THE SPECIFIC SCHOOLS IN MY AREA?**
See the Box on page 41 for some suggestions about learning about the schools in your area. You will probably also ask the people you meet — colleagues, neighbors, real estate or rental agents and others — about schools. Just remember that these sources of information may or may not be reliable, share your values, or be up to date. Some of these people may have no direct experience with the schools they recommend or with those they think are lacking. Even if they are parents, the educational goals and expectations they have for their children may be quite different from yours. Do your own research. An independent education consultant is often the best resource for providing an objective overview of all the schooling options available. An experienced consultant is familiar with a wide range of schools and works directly with families to identify the best possible match for each child.

**WHAT DO THESE COMPARATIVE STATISTICS MEAN?**
Comparative statistics about schools can be helpful, but they can also be confusing or, worse, misleading. Here is some background information about some of the statistics you will see:

**% seniors who go to four-year college:** In the U.S. as a whole, 66% of male high school graduates and 74% of female graduates go on to a four-year college or university. School districts often publish the percent of their seniors who do so. However, this statistic is often as much an indicator of the community's social class as it is of its schools' educational quality.

**SAT and ACT scores:** The Scholastic Aptitude Test (SAT) and the ACT (originally, the American College Testing program) are nationwide college admission tests that high school juniors and seniors take. The SAT tests Critical Reading (formerly called "Verbal"), Writing and Math skills; scores range from 200-800. For reference, the national average in the U.S. is about 501 (Critical Reading) 516 (Mathematics) and 494 (Writing). (Students may also take SAT Subject Tests, which assess achievement in subject areas like physics, history, literature, etc.) The ACT tests English, math, science reasoning, and reading. The highest possible score is 36; the national average is about 21. Some school districts encourage all high school seniors to take these tests (including some who will not go to college); in others, only the better students take them. Therefore, it may be difficult to interpret the meaning of the average scores in different districts.

**student expenditure:** States give each district some amount of money for education. Most of the rest of the education budget comes from local taxes. Local communities have very different tax rates and make very different decisions about how and where to spend their money. So it may be useful to look at the average amount of money spent per student in each district. For reference, the national average in the U.S. is about $10,600 (including costs of instruction, student support, administration and operations). However, research has not shown a very strong relation between per-student expenditure and academic achievement.

**teacher salary:** Comparing the salaries in neighboring communities is sometimes an indicator of the seniority of teachers and the value placed on public education. Private school teachers' salaries are generally lower than public school ones. The nation-

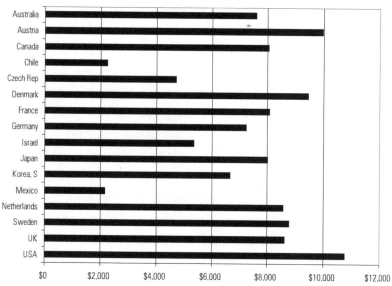

## Per-Student Expenditure

Australia
Austria
Canada
Chile
Czech Rep
Denmark
France
Germany
Israel
Japan
Korea, S
Mexico
Netherlands
Sweden
UK
USA

$0    $2,000    $4,000    $6,000    $8,000    $10,000    $12,000

*Source: Organization for Economic Co-operation and Development (OECD)*

al average public school teachers' salary is about $55,000; for private schools, it is about $41,000. However, the cost of living varies widely in the U.S. so you should be cautious when comparing your communities' salaries with national ones.

### CAN I VISIT A SCHOOL WHILE WE ARE TRYING TO CHOOSE?

Private schools encourage — or even insist on — parents and students to visit the school before applying. They will arrange tours and meetings for you with appropriate teachers and staff. Whenever possible, visit the schools you are considering with your children, talk with faculty and administrators, tour the campus and attend classes. Many schools have parent networks to assist new families; they can be helpful as you make your school choice. To arrange your visit, call the Admissions Office.

Public schools will also usually welcome a visit from you if you have serious plans to move into its neighborhood, and will certainly do so if you have signed a lease or bought a home. Call the main office (or principal's office, or guidance office) to arrange for a visit.

Whenever you visit a school — public or private — first report to the main office and introduce yourself. This is a matter of courtesy and safety, as the school has a responsibility to its students to know who is in the building at all times.

### WHAT SHOULD I LOOK FOR WHEN I VISIT A SCHOOL?

The objective in school selection is to find the best possible match between the needs of your child and the education provided by the school. Each child has a unique set of social needs, interests, and learning abilities, and each school offers a unique combination of teaching philosophy, size, curriculum, cost, and student body composition. Because of the number of factors to be considered and the difficulty in measuring these factors, the selection process can be demanding. Here are some guidelines to help you with your search:

**Ask for a meeting with someone (like a guidance counselor) who can answer your questions.**
- *Is this meeting easy or difficult to arrange?*
- *Does the school seem interested in your child's academic background and level, or will they make a class placement simply on the basis of age?*

**Do you like the philosophy of education and educational goals at this school?** Try to understand how it differs from what you have at home. It will surely be different. Unless you go to a school run by educators from your country, you should not look for an exact match of philosophy, because every country's education system is different. Instead, ask:

- *Would you like your child to have the experience of being in this particular system?*
- *Can your child benefit from being in this kind of school?*
- *Look in the school's written materials and statement of goals, and compare what you see in the class room with what you expect. Do you like what you see?*

**Are you confident about the quality of the school?** Public schools will be required to meet statewide quality standards; you can compare them using the criteria and statistics mentioned in this chapter. Private schools should be accredited by at least one respected accreditation board (see Box in Chapter 1). You should ask how long the school has been accredited and by whom.

- *How frequently is the school inspected, and by what agencies, to insure that proper academic standards are maintained?*
- *Does the school undergo periodic peer review?*
- *What are the student retention and attrition rates?*

**How big is the school?** What does this mean in terms of class size and available resources? Sometimes larger schools (private and public) can afford more extensive support and facilities than. smaller schools. On the other hand, some smaller schools effectively use connections in the community to make up for their small size.

- *What is the enrollment of the school?*
- *How big are the classes your child would be in? Do any teachers have helpers?*
- *What kinds of programs do they have for children who need extra help or extra challenge?*
- *What do the teachers do to challenge their students?*

- *What science, library, arts, and sports facilities will be available to the students?*

**Is there a "sense of community" at the school?** As you visit the school, ask yourself whether this school would be welcoming to your child, and whether he/she would feel included and valued.

- *Are there opportunities for students to participate in and contribute to the school community?*
- *Do students feel a sense of loyalty and enthusiasm about their school?*
- *Is the social climate of the school one that would be comfortable for your child?*
- *Is the student body homogeneous or diverse in terms of social, ethnic, religious, or nationality?*
- *What steps does the school take to welcome new students?*
- *Do parents play an active role in school affairs?*

**Do you feel confident of the leadership and faculty at the school?**

- *Has the head/principal set a positive and consistent tone for the school community?*
- *How long has the head/principal served at this school?*
- *Is the head/principal accessible and responsive to the school community?*
- *What are the backgrounds and credentials of the teachers?*
- *What is the background of the head/principal of the school?*

**What is the condition of the school building and grounds?** This can be an outer sign of the financial status of the school. Some suburban public schools and private boarding schools have very substantial "campuses." They include extensive laboratory and workshop facilities, playing fields, indoor swimming pools, theaters, computer centers and large libraries. At the other end of the spectrum are schools, often in rural areas or the inner cities, with outdated and overcrowded plants surviving on inadequate budgets and lacking in the critical support of the larger community. The quality of education offered by a particular school is not necessarily related to its physical appearance, but its condition can be a good indication of the financial health of the district or school.

- *Does it look as if there is enough money to keep the building in good shape?*
- *Does there appear to be enough money to pay the teachers well and support educational programs?*

**Are there other international children in the school?** If there are no (or very few) children from your culture in the school, your child may feel isolated, at least for a while. On the other hand, if there are many children from your culture, your child may be slower to learn English and to make American friends.

- *What is done to integrate newcomers from other countries into the school?*
- *Are there signs that the school values international diversity?*

**Will your child be helped to learn English?** If your child is not a native English speaker, how important is it for him/her to learn English?

- *Are there any teachers who speak your language at the school?*
- *Is there a bilingual program, or a class in English as a Second Language?*
- *Does the school have a well-developed philosophy about how to teach English while maintaining a child's continuing cognitive development and academic progress?*

**For private schools, what are the tuition, fees, and other costs?**

- *Is financial assistance available?*
- *Is there an extended or deferred payment program?*
- *Are tuition insurance plans available?*

**Other Questions**

- *Is the school in a convenient location? Will your child have any neighbors who go to this school?*
- *Does the school offer the curriculum/activities that your child wants and needs?*
- *Is there an after-school program?*
- *Does the school offer boarding facilities?*
- *Does the school provide transportation?*
- *Does the school provide food service?*
- *When was the school founded? (The founding date of a private school, combined with its length of accreditation, tells you something about the stability of the school.)*

If you have questions or worries (now or later) about school policies or services, be sure to ask. Do not expect to be told all that you need or want to know without asking. But do expect to have all your questions answered.

### HOW CAN I TELL IF THE SCHOOL WILL BE SAFE?

Tragic stories of violence in American schools have made international news and are understandably worrisome to newcomers. It is important to remember that these incidents, while horrible, are very rare. Schools have already responded in many ways. Many schools limit and monitor visitors' (including parents') presence very carefully. Some high schools have started to use metal detectors, like those in airports. Severe punishments are given to students who bring any kind of weapon to a school building and to those who threaten anyone, even if it is meant as a joke. Teachers and guidance counselors have received increased training in how to respond to children in need and to prevent bullying. If you ever have specific concerns about your child's safety, contact a teacher, guidance counselor, principal, or headmaster immediately.

## IT'S SO CONFUSING; HOW DO WE FINALLY DECIDE WHICH SCHOOL IS BEST?

In the end, you will have to weigh what you hear, the statistics, and the advice others give you along with your knowledge of your children, their past schooling, and what kinds of education they will need in their own futures. Use the School Comparison Worksheet on the next page to help organize your evaluations.

# School Comparison Worksheet

You have read an overview of the ways American schools differ from each other and from the schools in your home country. Now, your decision will be about your child, with his/her unique skills and needs, and about the few specific schools you are considering. Use this chart to help you compare the schools.

| | School #1 | School #2 | School #3 | School #4 | How important is this to you? (1 = not very important 5 = very important) |
|---|---|---|---|---|---|
| Do you like the values and methods used at the school? | | | | | |
| Do the teachers seem competent and happy? | | | | | |
| How good are the facilities that are most important to you (library, computers, sports, performing arts)? | | | | | |
| Would you like your child to be part of this group of students? | | | | | |
| What class size would your child have? | | | | | |
| Would your child receive the challenge and/or special help needed? | | | | | |
| Will your child be prepared to return to your home country after attending this school? | | | | | |
| Is the school convenient to your home? | | | | | |
| Can you afford this school? | | | | | |
| TOTAL (add each column) | | | | | |
| WEIGHTED TOTAL (Multiply each rating by your Importance rating in the right-hand column, and add these scores.) | | | | | |

CHAPTER 5
# Admissions and Enrollment

### HOW DO I ENROLL MY CHILD IN A PUBLIC SCHOOL?

Because any child living in a school district may attend that school for free, there is no admissions procedure for public schools. To enroll, simply call the school to set up an appointment to meet with the principal or guidance counselor. Depending on the size and structure of the school, some other administrative office may handle the paperwork, but it's a good idea to begin with the principal and his or her assistant. Bring the materials listed in the Box below. The necessary paperwork can be completed at the school. Copies are then sent on to the district offices.

---

#### SCHOOL REGISTRATION: WHAT TO BRING

- [ ] proof of child's birth date (passport),
- [ ] school records and work samples from the past two years, to help with placement into the most appropriate class,
- [ ] proof that you live in your community (lease, purchase and sale agreement, or state driver's license; be sure your proof has your street address printed on it), and
- [ ] medical and immunization records (see next page for details).

---

### HOW DOES MY CHILD APPLY TO A PRIVATE SCHOOL?

Private schools typically have limited space. They often try to admit groups of highly qualified students of varied backgrounds and interests. Many of these schools cannot admit all the qualified students who apply. The application process is often detailed and can take several months to complete. Application deadlines may be as early as January for the following September. After the deadline, schools may consider new applicants only if spaces

## IMMUNIZATION REQUIREMENTS

Children entering any preschool, school, or college will have to show a record of their immunizations. Countries differ in their recommended immunization schedules. Go to www.cdc.gov/vaccines for a description of the immunizations recommended in the U.S. for babies, children, adolescents and adults.

To enroll in a U.S. school, your child will have to comply with the U.S. recommended immunization schedule. Do not assume that the immunizations your child received in your home country will be sufficient for entering an American school. Each state sets its own rules about immunizations but most require immunization against:

Diphtheria
Tetanus
Pertussis
Hepatitis B
Polio
Measles
Mumps
Rubella
Varicella
Haemophilus influenza (Hib)

Children may also need to show that they have had a lead screening test, as lead in the blood has been found to cause learning problems in young children.

Go to www.immunizationinfo.org/vaccines/state-requirements for a list of each state's requirements for school entry. Requirements change fairly frequently so do not rely on information that may be out of date.

If your child has not had the immunizations required by state law, you must arrange for these shots to be given before starting school. Your pediatrician or school nurse will tell you how to have your child immunized safely to meet the state requirements. Some schools may require that your child be examined by a U.S. physician prior to starting school so that this physician may complete necessary paperwork.

are still available. Private schools may choose not to accept applications for admission in the middle of a school year.

To begin the application process, call the "head of school" (for smaller schools) or the Admissions Office. The following steps are normally required:

1. Some type of entrance exam will usually be required. In some cases the school may accept a standardized test such as the SSAT (Secondary School Admission Test) or they may prefer to administer their own.

2. Admission interviews are highly recommended and are often required by a school before it will officially admit a student.

3. The following documentation is usually required:

   a. the application form itself,

   b. application fee in the form of a personal check,

   c. names and addresses of previous schools attended; dates of attendance,

   d. transcripts: copies of course lists, grades and evaluations for at least two years,

   e. two letters from teachers addressing the child's abilities, character, and achievements,

   f. examples of your child's work, including samples of completed math and English assignments,

   g. some sample assignments that show the level of your child's current work,

   h. medical records, including immunization history and results of a recent, full physical examination,

   i. birth certificate, passport and visa (the latter two for non-U.S. citizens), and

   j. any testing information that reflects your child's ability or special needs.

It may be useful to have some of these materials translated into

English and to include an explanation of your home country's grading and educational system.

## CAN I ENROLL MY CHILDREN IN SCHOOL IF THEY HAVE NOT YET COME TO THE U.S.?

Once you have proof that you have a residence in a community (like an apartment lease or purchase and sale agreement on a house) you can begin the registration process for a public school. However, most private schools will require an on-site campus interview with your child and most require a day spent on the campus. Some schools will hold a space for a student if all the paperwork looks acceptable and the interview is the only outstanding piece of the process.

## HOW WILL THE SCHOOL DETERMINE WHAT CLASS AND LEVEL TO PLACE MY CHILD IN?

Besides the child's age and English ability, both public and private schools may consider current and past school report cards and teacher references. Most private schools will conduct some testing, especially in language arts and math, to assess grade levels. Private schools' admission testing also helps with placement.

## WHAT SHOULD I EXPLAIN TO THE SCHOOL ABOUT MY HOME COUNTRY'S EDUCATION SYSTEM AND MY CHILD'S OWN LEARNING HISTORY?

Most schools, both public and private, do NOT have a very good understanding about other countries' education systems. It will be very important for you to educate your new school — especially your child's teacher — about the differences in teaching and grading methods, subjects taught, educational goals, behavior, and expectations. Spend a little time explaining the level of your child's previous course work. Your new U.S. school may not be familiar with the competitive nature of your home country academics. You may want to mention, for example, if, in your country, it is the exceptional student who is selected to take pre-university studies.

**HOW CAN I BE SURE THE SCHOOL UNDERSTANDS MY CHILD'S TRANSCRIPT FROM HOME?**

There are independent organizations that evaluate educational documents from other countries. In most cases, if your documents are in another language, you must first have the documents translated into English by an independent company (not yourself). Then you supply the evaluating agency with an official copy of the translated documents. One such company is World Education Services (www.wes.org).

Such an evaluation serves to "translate" your child's educational record in two ways — first from your home language into English, and then from your system into the American one. For example, a "B" in one country may actually be equivalent to an "A" in the U.S. For students who have already done university level work, evaluation services can do a credit by credit analysis of the work done, providing a report that "translates" the information from one country's system to another.

CHAPTER 6

# *The Early Years*

CAN MY CHILD GO TO SCHOOL BEFORE KINDERGARTEN?

Growing numbers of parents in the U.S. send their 3- and 4-year-old children to *preschools*, although the enrollment rates are still lower than in many countries (see Chart below). The vast majority of these programs are private (so you will have to pay for them). You may choose any preschool you like, regardless of where you live, as long as it has space. You will find religion-based preschools, Montessori Schools, private nursery schools and day-care programs, and pre-kindergartens (PK) that are part of PK-8 (primary) or PK-12 (comprehensive) private schools.

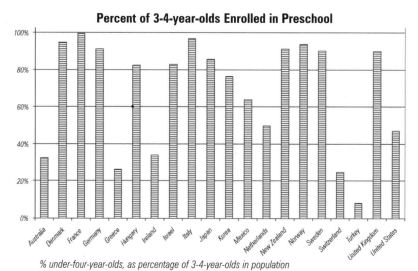

**Percent of 3-4-year-olds Enrolled in Preschool**

*% under-four-year-olds, as percentage of 3-4-year-olds in population*

Source: Organization for Economic Co-operation and Development (OECD)

Preschool daily schedules vary considerably. They may provide morning, afternoon and/or full-day programs. Annual costs range from $3,800 to $10,900 (average $8,700) and may be higher if parents choose extended hours, if there are specialty programs at the school, and/or in some regions of the country. Preschool is not a requirement in any state. (However, an increasing number of public school districts offer early childhood programs; ask about these in the school district you are considering.)

### WHAT SHOULD I KNOW ABOUT CHOOSING A PRESCHOOL?

It is very important for parents to check the credentials and licensing of any preschool and its staff. Catholic pre-schools and many independent pre-schools that are part of an elementary or secondary school will be accredited. Other private nursery schools and day-care centers may not be required to be accredited in the same fashion, but be sure that they are licensed and approved according to your state's guidelines.

Make an appointment to visit several preschools, tour the facilities and interview the staff members who will be working with your children. If the preschool is in a church or temple, ask if religion is a part of the activity of the preschool. Sometimes it is, but often it is not.

Preschools are often filled well in advance of opening day, especially in big cities. It's never too early to investigate preschool options — parents often inquire about placing a child in a preschool a full year in advance of the planned starting date. Enrollment generally works on a rolling basis — that is, children are accepted as they apply until the class is full.

Many state Departments of Education keep track of the preschools within their boundaries and will provide information to interested parents. Find your state's education website by doing a search for your state's name and "department of education."

## CHOOSING A PRESCHOOL FOR YOUR CHILD

There are probably many excellent licensed preschools in your area, but they may be very different from each other. Your job will be to find the school that is best for your child and that provides the kind of preschool experience you think is best. Some educators think the best preschools are ones that give children a free choice from among many safe and stimulating materials and activities. Play itself is seen as the method of education. Other preschools offer a more structured approach to learning, with lessons in letters, numbers, and basic concepts. Within this broad range of views, try to watch for:

- a school in which the "energy level" would be a match for your child (some children need lots of time to run around and make noise; others need lots of time for quiet play),

- a school in which the "schedule" would be a match for your child (some children like predictability and others get very upset if they have to stop doing something fun to do the next thing on the schedule),

- teachers who are skilled at bringing new children into the group,

- teachers who clearly know the individual needs and styles of the different children in the school and adapt their teaching to these different styles,

- ways in which the school addresses children's different developmental needs: emotional, social, cognitive, school-readiness, and physical,

- appropriate concerns for health and safety, including rules about hand-washing, giving medication, safe playground play, fire drills, toy cleanliness, and safe indoor spaces, and

- a reasonable level of involvement of the teachers with the children (children need some time to play alone and among themselves to develop socially, but even then, teachers should be actively supervising and watching the play).

It is a good idea to look at several preschools before choosing one. Talk with the director, and spend some time there with your child. While good preschools are open to parent visits at any time, as a courtesy you should call ahead to schedule an appointment, even after your child is enrolled.

# CHAPTER 7

# Daily Customs and Practical Issues

## WHEN WILL MY CHILD GO TO SCHOOL?

American students generally go to school Mondays through Fridays for about 6 hours per day. Some kindergartens are only three or four hours per day. There is a lot of variation from school to school, both in the exact number of hours and in the timing of the day. The length of the American school day may be very different from what your child has experienced in your home country. The American day may feel unusually long or unusually short! Sports and other extracurricular afternoon programs are usually held in the afternoons after regular school hours.

The school year begins in late August or early September and runs at least until mid- to late May, typically into the latter half of June. Public schools in most states are currently required to provide a minimum of 180 days of instruction per school year. Private schools generally schedule approximately 170 school days.

Vacation schedules vary among schools even in the same geographical area. Public and private school vacation schedules may differ significantly. However, in both kinds of schools, there is usually a vacation of one to two weeks during the last week of December to the first week of January. All schools also have some kind of late winter or early spring break. There is substantial variation among schools and districts. A recent trend in some regions has been toward a week of vacation in the latter part of February and another week in April. Other holidays of one to two days occur throughout the year. You will receive a calendar of holidays when you register your child at school.

**Days of School per Year**

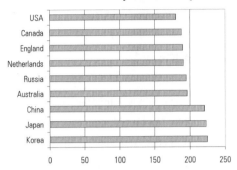

Source: Trends in International Mathematics and Science Study (TIMSS)

Boarding schools tend to have longer winter and spring vacations and fewer one- and two-day holidays, to meet the needs of students who live far away. The longer vacations let students return home for longer periods and decrease the number of holidays they might have to remain on campus when school is not in session.

A great deal of discussion has recently focused on proposed changes in the school year schedule. The long summer vacation was historically for farm families who needed their children to work in the fields during the summer. Some schools are now reconsidering the schedule in light of modern concerns. For example, some are planning ways to teach students in "shifts" throughout the year (in groups at different times) so they can make more efficient use of the building and facilities during the summer. Although rare, some districts may offer families a choice between a nine-month or year-round school calendar.

## WORDS TO KNOW

**Open House**
A night when parents come to the school (maybe with their children, maybe alone) to meet the teacher, visit the classroom, and hear about the plans for the year.

**Field Trip**
A class trip away from the school. May cost extra money (for bus travel, admission fees, or snacks).

**Permission Slip**
A form to be signed by a parent, giving permission to do a special activity and/or go on a field trip.

**Excused Absence**
Some schools require that parents write a short note to explain why a child missed school (for example, "Dear Ms. Lee, Please excuse Eva's absence from school on Thursday as she was sick. Sincerely, Anke Herzog"). Other schools require parents to call them by telephone to say if their child will be absent that day.

**Homeroom**
In grades when children move from one classroom to another for different subjects, this is the room (and group of children and teacher) in which they hear announcements.

**Parent-Teacher Organization**
Organization that serves as liaison between school and home. May hold meetings, fund-raisers, receptions, lectures.

**Show and Tell**
In younger grades, there may be a regular time during the week for children to show something (like a picture of a grandparent who visited, or a postcard from a friend) or tell about something (a trip to the zoo, a recent soccer game) to the class.

**Report Card or Conference Report**
A written notice about a child's progress in different subjects in school. Report cards are usually sent home 2-4 times a year. Conference reports are usually given to parents following a parent-teacher conference about the child's progress. Increasingly, grade reports of all kinds are posted on line. Parents cants establish a password to view their child's grades for homework and tests on a regular basis so they can keep track of how their child is performing.

**Recess**
A time during the school day for (younger) children to play outside.

**School Handbook**
A booklet that lists all school rules and procedures.

## WHAT CAN MY CHILDREN DO DURING
## THE LONG SUMMER VACATION?

Many families use some of the summer holiday to take a vacation together. The rest of the time, children can:

- go to a "day camp" (a summer program that children attend during the day; day camps may include a variety of sports and crafts activities or may specialize in a sport, computers, arts, etc.; they usually have nothing to do with "camping"),

- go to a "sleepover" or "overnight camp" (a summer program where children stay in tents or cabins, usually from one to eight weeks),

- go to a summer educational program (many colleges offer summer enrichment programs for middle and high school students),

- get a job (many high school students work during the summer; states have different age limits so be sure to ask),

- go to summer school at the school they attend during the year (these can be very useful for relocating families as a low-pressure introduction to the American school system and to the English language, when necessary), or

- play at home (but ask about your own neighborhood; many newcomers report surprise at how few available friends there are in the summer).

## I WORK FULL TIME. WHAT ARE THE OPTIONS FOR
## MY CHILD AFTER REGULAR SCHOOL HOURS?

Some elementary schools offer an after-school care program in their building. Parents have to pay for this, although sometimes scholarships are available. Some communities offer after-school care programs in town recreation centers or other convenient locations. Bus transportation may be available. In other cases, parents put together an assortment of after-school music lessons, play dates with friends, and sports teams so that their children are

## After-School Activities in the U.S., Kindergarten-8th Grade

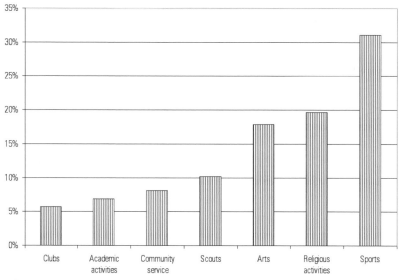

Source: The Condition of Education

not left alone in the afternoon. Some families hire after-school babysitters if the parents cannot be present themselves. Although most states do not have laws about when a child may be left alone, some states do require that a child be of a certain age in order to be without supervision.

### HOW WILL MY CHILD GET TO SCHOOL?

Most American children get to school by walking, bicycle, school bus, car, or public transportation. If you live close enough that your children can walk or ride a bicycle, you will have to decide if it is safe for them to go alone or if you or an older child should go with them. Consider the amount of traffic, whether there will be a crossing guard at busy intersections, and the general safety of the route. All children must wear an approved bicycle helmet when riding a bicycle in the U.S. Ask at the school whether it is advisable to lock a bicycle on the school grounds.

Public school systems may offer free school bus transportation if you live far enough from the school. (The required distance varies from district to district.) Private schools often provide bus service for their students for a fee. Typically, the younger the child, the closer the school bus stop is to his or her home. Sometimes, children will need to make a bus transfer before arriving at their school; these arrangements are all organized by the school district's transportation department. The school will explain everything you need to know about pick-up and drop-off and the bus schedule. *Be sure your child understands where to get the bus at school, where to get off coming home, and exactly what to do if he/she misses the bus, either going to school or coming home.* This is especially important in the early days, particularly if your child's English is not yet strong.

In some states, the public school system will provide bus transportation for private school students living within 15 miles of the school they attend. And in some cases busing for disabled students attending private schools up to fifty miles away is paid for by the public schools.

It may be appropriate for your child to take public transportation to school. Again, you will have to decide if this is safe and appropriate for your child. Usually a student discount rate is available.

Parents often drop off or pick up their children by car. Many families form car pools, sharing the responsibility of driving their children to and from school with one or a few other families. American students may apply for a driving permit at the age of 16-18 (depending on the state). In some communities, many high school students drive to school.

**DOES IT MATTER WHAT MY CHILD WEARS TO SCHOOL?**

Parochial schools, some private schools, and a very few public schools require that students wear a uniform. Skirts for girls and coats and ties for boys are traditional. Those attending public schools or the less conservative independent schools are generally free to dress as they choose. Schools may have a formal or informal "dress code" with some rules for dressing in a way that encourages productive studying. See your school's handbook for your school's rules.

The dress code of public school children may be different from what you have in your home country. Most students chose very informal attire. They dress either for comfort or to make a fashion statement or both, but almost always very casually.

**WHAT WILL MY CHILD EAT FOR LUNCH?**

American children usually eat lunch at school. Many, but not all, schools offer a hot lunch for sale. Your child may have to bring money every day to buy the school lunch. Other schools allow parents to pre-pay for the month, semester, or year; some have an online system in which parents may "refill" a child's lunch account using a credit card, so that neither parents nor students have to carry cash or checks to school. Or your child can bring a lunch from home. Children from families with low incomes can get their lunches free or at a lower cost; the school will explain how to apply for this when you register. The funding for this reduced-rate lunch comes from the federal government. To get this federal money, each school district is supposed to make sure that the lunches are nutritious. There are rules about nutritional value and fat content. But the schools also try to make food that children like, with varying success.

Your child may prefer to bring lunch from home and/or buy a drink or dessert at school. Your child's choice will depend on personal family finances, food likes and dislikes, what other students at school do, and his/her age. Lunch, and the recess that typically follows it, are important opportunities for school children to socialize.

**WHAT SHOULD MY CHILD DO IF THE CLASS IS EXPECTED TO RECITE THE "PLEDGE OF ALLEGIANCE?"**

Students in some American public schools recite "The Pledge of Allegiance" to the American flag (see Box). You or your child may feel uncomfortable with this ritual. Discuss with your child (and, if necessary, the teacher or guidance counselor) how to show respect without necessarily conforming fully to this school tradition.

---

**Here are the words to the Pledge of Allegiance:**

*I pledge allegiance to the flag of the United States of America,*

*And to the Republic for which it stands,*

*One nation under God, indivisible,*

*With liberty and justice for all.*

---

**WHAT SHOULD I DO IF MY CHILD IS SICK?**

In general, American schools prefer you to keep your children at home if they are sick, to speed their recovery and avoid infecting other children. Some schools have guidelines to help you know whether your child is too sick to go to school. For example, they may say to keep your child at home if he/she :

- has had a fever within the last 24 hours,
- has recently vomited or had diarrhea more than once,
- has frequent coughing, or any other disruptive symptoms, or

- is still in the contagious period of a disease (like chicken pox).

If you are unsure what to do, ask your child's doctor or school nurse.

Many American public schools require parents to report all school absences at the beginning of the school day, and/or write a note explaining the absence when the child returns. If parents do not do so, they may be called at home to verify the absence. Ask about the rules at your child's school.

CHAPTER 8
# *Academic Curriculum*

## WHAT WILL MY CHILD STUDY?

There is no national curriculum in the U.S., so it is difficult to say specifically what your child will study at each age. Although teachers have some choice in what topics to teach, the curriculum is generally designed by the local school district, which oversees the coherence of the program. Very generally:

- Kindergarten is usually considered a time to "prepare to learn." Some kindergarten classes are quite open and free, allowing children to experience a rich variety of social relationships and learning tasks as they choose to do so. Others have a more structured curriculum for teaching. Most begin to introduce basic letters and numbers, and to emphasize social concepts that will prepare children for school: cooperation, sharing, and planning. Most American kindergarten teachers consider children's "play" to be a very important way of learning. Through play children use and learn about their senses, how to resolve conflicts, how to experiment with and apply concepts, and so on. While some children will come to kindergarten already reading, the emphasis for most children will be on "reading readiness" — learning letters and sounds, listening to a story, building vocabulary, and understanding the concept of sequence.

- In the first three elementary (or primary) school years, children will learn to read and write, and begin to practice accurate spelling. They will learn to print letters, write in cursive, and begin to learn "keyboarding" (typing) on a computer. Children will learn to master simple arithmetic and begin to learn multiplication tables. They will begin to apply these basic skills to the study of "social studies," which includes history, anthropology, economics, geography, sociology, art history, and politics. They explore some basic scientific concepts and the scientific method: hypothesizing, testing, observing, evaluating, interpreting.

- In the later elementary years, children are expected to have mastered reading, handwriting, and basic arithmetic skills. They continue to get specific instruction in vocabulary, spelling, comprehension, and writing (composition) skills. They are exposed to a variety of literary forms. They begin to study percentage, ratio, decimals, and the application of math to real-life problems. Social studies and science concepts are now approached in more depth, giving the children the experience of having a more detailed understanding in a few areas. For example, students may spend several months studying "the ancient world" of Egypt, Africa, and Mesopotamia, or a month studying "optics," integrating different subject content around such a central theme. They will also usually study American history and the history of their own state.

- In middle school, the major subjects are taught in more depth. Students begin to study algebra, earth and physical sciences, and literature. In some school districts, foreign languages are taught for the first time in the middle school years. Art, music, and physical education are typically taught once or twice a week. All children in a middle school will study the same subjects (except they may have some choice among foreign languages), regardless of their ability. Some schools have "advanced" classes in math, science, and/or language arts for children who have excelled in these areas.

## Languages Offered by U.S. High Schools with Language Programs

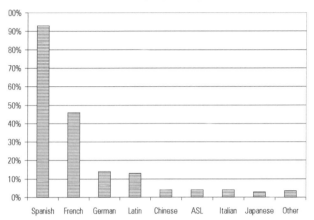

Note: Over 90% U.S. high schools offer foreign language instruction. About 43% students in U.S. high schools study a foreign language.

Source: Center for Applied Linguistics

- In high school, most students continue to study the major academic subjects of science, math, English (literature and writing), social studies, and a foreign language. Students often study one type of science for a whole year: biology, chemistry, physics. They study world history one year, and American history another. Depending on the student's ability and interest, he/she may study algebra, geometry, trigonometry, and/or pre-calculus. Many high schools offer two or three different levels (of difficulty or challenge) of most of these courses. Students usually are required to take a Health and Fitness, or physical education class. Many schools also offer a variety of "elective" courses (like cooking, wood-working, painting, or chorus) which students may elect to take. There may also be specific requirements set by the state or school district for the study of such topics as state history, government and civics, or driver education. See Chapter 10 for more information on high school curricular issues.

## What 8th Graders Do During Math Class

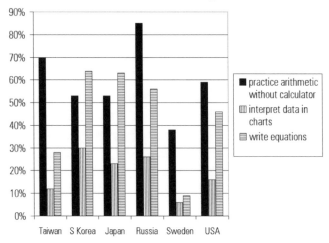

Note: Based on teachers' reports of whether students do the following activities about half of the lessons or more: practice arithmetic without using a calculator; interpret data in tables, charts or graphs; and write equations and functions to represent relationships.

Source: Trends in International Mathematics and Sciences Study

I HAVE HEARD THAT AMERICAN STUDENTS DO NOT SCORE VERY WELL ON MATH AND SCIENCE TESTS. HOW CAN I BE SURE MY CHILD LEARNS MATH AND SCIENCE?

Some recent international comparisons of math and science knowledge have raised this concern. These tests were a wake-up call to American educators and many reforms have been put into place to try to change how these subjects are taught. To put the scores in perspective, however, it is important to remember that the range in Americans' scores was very large — there were some very high and some very low scores. The range in scores probably reflects a number of factors, including a range in the quality of schools. If your children will be going to one of the better schools, they will probably be getting better instruction in math and science. Student scores for the best American schools compare very favorably with those from other countries.

## How to Teach "The 3 R's"

You may hear Americans refer to "the 3 R's." This is simply a "cute" way of describing the three fundamental academic skills: "readin', writin', and 'rithmetic." Across the U.S., you will find many different approaches to the teaching of reading, spelling, and math:

**Reading:**   Some teachers emphasize the teaching of phonics, or the matching of sounds and letters so that children can learn to sound out new words. Others use the "Look Say" method, teaching children to recognize, on sight, a whole word. Most children probably learn to read using a combination of these methods, leaning one way or the other based on their learning style and training. The "Whole Language" approach involves addressing reading as part of the whole language area of reading, writing, and speaking. Teachers provide a variety of language-based activities — talking and writing about books, feelings, and experiences.

**Spelling:**   Some teachers, at least in the first several grades, encourage "inventive spelling," letting children spell words as they sound ("gd" for "good"). The theory is that, with experience and later training, children will begin to spell correctly; but in the meantime, they will have continued to write freely and creatively about their world, unburdened by the demand to spell correctly.

**Math:**   Especially in light of recent disappointing scores on international comparisons of students' math abilities, American teachers have been trying to develop improved ways of teaching math. The question has been how much to emphasize rote memorization, drill, and computational skills, and how much to emphasize higher mathematical thinking, problem solving, estimation, learning through manipulation of objects, and application to real-life problems. This is a continuing debate.

In addition, at least until recently, American math and science curricula, with their emphasis on hands-on learning and conceptual problem-solving, perhaps did not prepare students for the kinds of questions asked on the international tests. It is reassuring that, in international comparisons of adult literacy through adulthood, American adults' quantitative scores compare well with those in other countries. Still, you may want to discuss math and science approaches with your children's school, to be sure they are in the most challenging courses, and/or to supplement the school's teaching with extra classes or tutoring.

### SOME TOPICS SEEM TO BE TAUGHT IN TOO MUCH DETAIL, WHILE OTHERS ARE ONLY GIVEN LIGHT TREATMENT; WHY?

American teachers sometimes choose one narrow topic (like "wolves" or "Beethoven") to study in detail. Why wolves, not "mammals?" Why Beethoven, not "composers?" By teaching a single topic in detail, teachers are trying to give students a sense of how to study a topic in depth, integrating such notions as habitat, migration, and the interconnected web of life. On the other hand, in the American system, many important topics (like "decimals" or "medieval history") are taught at several different ages, in increasing detail and sophistication. What seems to be "light treatment" may be just the first introduction of a topic that will be taught again and again over several years.

### WHAT KIND OF COMPUTER TRAINING SHOULD WE EXPECT?

Almost every American school and classroom has Internet access. On average, you will find one computer for every 3.9 students. About 95% of U.S. schools have high-speed Internet access and about one third have a wireless network. Keyboarding (typing) is an increasingly common part of the elementary school curriculum. Students will learn to use the Internet to do research in all subject areas. They may also learn web design and programming.

### WHAT IF MY CHILD DOES NOT SPEAK ENGLISH?

Many public schools offer a free ESL (English as a Second Language) program to students who, as measured by testing,

English Learners in U.S. Schools: A Look at the Numbers

**22.2%** U.S. students have at least one **foreign-born parent**.

About **21%** U.S. students **speak a language other than English at home**. The number is highest in the West (33%) and lowest in the Midwest (11%).

**33** states have standards for English Language Learner teachers; **3** states require all prospective teachers to be competent in ELL instruction; **11** states offer incentives to teachers to earn ELL expertise; **7** states ban or restrict native-language instruction.

*Source: U.S. Census Bureau and National Center for Education Statistics*

need it. In your school system, ESL may be referred to as ELL (English Language Learning), EAL (English as an Additional Language) or a similar other name. ESL programs are often set up as "pull-outs." This means that the students will be placed in regular classes according to their age and attend these classes with their peers, even though they may initially understand very little of what is said. They may be "pulled out" of the normal class cycle for a while to attend an ESL class led by a certified ESL teacher. ESL teachers are trained to teach English to non-native speakers regardless of what the student's first language is. Do not expect that your child's ESL teacher will speak your language.

ESL students are expected to participate in all of their regular (non-ESL) classes and to do the assigned work. However, grades in most regular coursework are generally not given during the first semester or until a certain level of language comprehension has been reached. ESL programs provide essential language training and give foreign students a place to be comfortable during the initial adjustment period without isolating them from the rest of school community.

ESL may be provided in different ways in different school systems. Not all programs are "pull-outs." Indeed, recent research indicates that students learning a new language often fare best when they remain in ongoing contact with peers who already speak the target language. An effort is being made by many districts to provide ESL teachers who join students in their classes in order to work with them on their regular coursework. This enables students to remain integrated into the greater fabric of their school and with students in their grade throughout the day. This approach is usually used when a student already speaks English fairly well.

In some districts, ESL remains a very separate entity, and students are not only pulled out of their regular classes but are also transported to a separate facility where ESL is provided to all of the children in a district who need it. In such instances, the goal is to have students return to their "home" school for regular schooling as soon as their English level permits it. Overall, it is important to ask a school or a district official how ESL will be "delivered" in a given school and grade level.

Schools may offer one of several kinds of *bilingual programs* (that is, programs that teach both in English and the student's native language). The goal of *maintenance bilingual programs* is to continue reading, writing, and speaking in both English and the student's first language. The goal of *transitional bilingual programs* is to learn in both languages only until the child knows English; then classes are all in English. The goal of *two-way bilingual programs* is to teach two languages to all students, both native English-speakers and newcomers to English.

Private schools are not required to provide ESL or bilingual training. However, a few do and others will admit foreign students for whom English is a second language and then help the family arrange private language tutoring. The cost of such programs is not included in the school's tuition fee.

You may want to begin intensive English language tutoring before moving to the U.S. Such lessons reinforce any language instruction your child may be getting in school and ease the transition into an English-speaking school. Some families also report that watching television helps their children learn English. Many television shows offer a closed caption text option, in which the words spoken on the show are displayed at the bottom of the screen. This may also help English learning.

### WILL THE SCHOOL HELP MY CHILDREN MAINTAIN THEIR NATIVE LANGUAGE?

In public school districts with many international newcomers from a particular language group, schools may offer bilingual education, although the emphasis in most of these programs is on preparing the child to study exclusively in English. Other schools offer such support informally, helping children maintain their native language skills and preparing them to return to their home country school system. These services are often organized in conjunction with an independent language school or an individual tutor. Some schools, usually private ones, will help families to organize and run special language or home curriculum tutoring.

### WHAT CAN I DO TO HELP MY CHILD LEARN ENGLISH?

- Continue to speak your native language at home, even if you are strongly committed to learning English. Children will more easily learn a second language if they are strong in a first.

- Continue to read to your child in your native language. You will be helping your child be a strong language learner, and will be sharing your home culture at the same time.

- At the same time, be a role model for learning English for your children. By speaking English some of the time — for example, in stores or at school — you will be showing your children that you think learning English is a good thing to do, and that making mistakes is OK. (But remember the first tip in this list, too.)

- Look for ways your child can practice English with one or two other people. It feels less risky to speak English to one person than to a group. Try arranging a play date with an English-speaking child.

- Understand that children often have a "silent period" when they first try English, or a time when they will not speak English. Be patient. They are learning to understand English, even if they are not speaking it. Forcing a child to speak can have negative effects on how fast they learn English.

- Remember that young children who are learning two languages at once are processing both languages, and may appear to be slower at speaking and reading than their friends. Don't panic. They are doing something more difficult. The reward will be knowing two languages.

- Realize that it takes up to seven years to learn a language well. Your child may be speaking English competently within six months or a year, but to function fully in school (or for you, in your adult life), it takes much longer.

- Understand that there is an emotional aspect to learning a second language. If learning English has a positive tone to it (for example, if your children want to learn, they think their parents are happy about learning English, and English has pleasant associations to it) learning will be faster. Do not pressure your children or be critical of how quickly they are learning English.

### WHAT SHOULD I DO IF THE SCHOOL DOES NOT SEEM CHALLENGING ENOUGH FOR MY CHILD?

Public schools may offer "pull-out" programs, enrichment in the classroom, independent study programs and the opportunity to take honors, Advanced Placement, or seminar courses, generally at the secondary level. Students may be selected for these special programs based on classroom performance, IQ tests, achievement test scores, and teacher recommendation.

Private schools may offer similar options. The more competitive schools tend not to differentiate as much among their students because they have already selected the academically talented ones through their admission processes.

There are also many exciting summer programs, often run through colleges and universities, that provide fun academic challenges to middle and high school students.

If your child does not seem to be challenged, talk with the teacher, a guidance counselor or advisor about other options.

### WHAT SHOULD I DO IF MY CHILD NEEDS SPECIAL HELP?

All public schools offer some kind of counseling and support services. Guidance counselors and/or school psychologists help students with school-related adjustment concerns, choosing courses and making post-graduate plans for further education, career development or job placement.

Federal law requires that public school districts accommodate all students, including those with special needs (like learning disabilities, visual and hearing impairments, mental retardation, and physical handicaps). Over 13% of public school children receive some kind of special education under the Individuals with Disabilities Act: for specific learning disabilities, speech or language impairments, intellectual disability, emotional disturbance, hearing or visual impairments, and others. Many schools have specialists trained to work with students who have learning or developmental differences. If your child's teacher thinks it is appropriate, she may suggest that your child be reviewed for possible evaluation of learning difficulties. The school is not allowed to do any special, formal testing without explaining to you why they think it is necessary and getting your written agreement.

Or, you can be the one to suggest that the school evaluate your child. Do this in writing, to the principal. Whether the recommendation for an evaluation comes from you or the school, you can always pay to have your child evaluated by a private psychologist and send the findings to the school.

If the results of the testing show that your child could benefit from extra or specialized help, you and a team of teachers and specialists will meet to review the testing results and other information, and to approve a plan (called an Individualized Education Program, or IEP). With your written permission, your child may be given extra help within the classroom, or may be given extra time or support during exams. Or he/she may leave the regular classroom several times a week to work with a specialist in another part of the school building. Or, in some cases, he/she may be placed in a special class for all or most of the day, along with other children with similar learning difficulties. Once a program has begun, the IEP must be reviewed at least once a year. See www2.ed.gov/parents/needs/speced/iepguide/ for information for parents about the IEP system.

Not all public schools can offer a full range of specialized services. If a school district finds, through testing and evaluation, that a student cannot be adequately taught within the school district, it may refer the student to an approved private school or to another public school outside the district. In either case the child's home school district must pay all costs, including transportation to the school.

Private schools do not attempt to serve all types of students. The more academic of them often specialize in preparing their students to compete for admission to the most selective colleges and universities. While some of these may offer special services for children with learning difficulties, others either do not admit them or require parents to provide the special services outside the school program. On the other hand, some private schools accept only students with learning differences or special education needs and may be better equipped to work with them than the public schools. Private schools have the advantage of being able to develop a focused educational mission and to select their students. They hire only the counselors or specialists appropriate to their particular programs and goals.

## How will I learn about my child's academic progress?

Many international parents of young children are surprised that they do not receive class ranking or formal grades. In the early years, most American educators take a "developmental approach" to evaluation, looking for signs of individual growth in skill and knowledge, rather than evaluation against some absolute standard or comparison with other children. You may be invited to a parent-teacher conference to review your child's progress. Areas of strength will be noted, as will areas that need improvement. But you will probably not get any indication of how your children compare to other students until they reach middle school or high school.

Schools differ in the age at which formal grades are given, but usually by middle school, children start to get formal report cards with grades in each subject two to four times per year. They may also get mid-term informal reports from each teacher. Grades reflect performance on tests, homework, and sometimes class participation. Schools often set a quality criterion and students who meet it are placed on an Honor Roll. Some schools also have an Effort Honor Roll, to reward effort.

---

**Most (though not all) American schools that give grades use the following system:**

A (the top grade; some schools also give A+)

A-

B+

B

B-

C+

C

C-

D (lowest passing grade)

F (failing grade; student will not receive credit for this course)

---

WHY IS CLASS PARTICIPATION SEEN AS SO IMPORTANT?

International families from some countries are surprised at the American emphasis on speaking in class, as opposed to listening to the teacher lecture. In the American system, discussion of ideas and putting thoughts into words are highly valued. Children are taught to speak aloud in class from the earliest days of kindergarten. They have "Show and Tell" or "Sharing Time," when each child is expected to speak to the whole class about something that has happened in their lives (a trip to the zoo, a visit from a grandmother, etc.) This skill at speaking becomes especially important in later years, as children are expected to ask questions, think creatively about solutions (even if the solutions are wrong!), and to disagree respectfully with the teacher. The American value of individualism is taught in this way.

WHAT ARE "STANDARDIZED TESTS"
AND HOW WILL THEY BE USED?

Standardized tests are tests that have been given all over the U.S. to thousands of children in each grade level, so their scores are called "standard." Most schools in the U.S. give children some of these tests in the middle elementary school years, and in junior and senior high school. Children typically take these tests in groups, usually in their classrooms. Test scores are used to evaluate educational policies and also the performance of specific districts and schools. Teachers look at them to see if there are surprises in their students' performance. If there are big gaps between the scores and the child's work, they may suggest that the child have more testing. Special class placements for children are not made on the basis of these group test scores alone.

Some schools always give the results of these tests to parents. Others do not, but, by law, you may always ask to see them.

There are three kinds of standardized tests:

- *Achievement tests* are supposed to measure how well a child has learned school subjects. There may be sub-tests of Reading, Mathematics, Language (spelling and grammar), Science, and Social Studies.

- *Ability tests* (sometimes called aptitude tests) are supposed to measure a child's potential to learn. But we know that all learning builds on itself. A child who has learned a lot in the past will do better on ability tests than a child who has not. Ability tests measure broader, more general skills (like logic and problem-solving) than achievement tests.

- *Basic Skills tests* are also common in many states. These tests are supposed to ensure that all children in a grade have certain basic skills before they go to the next higher grade.

When you look at your child's report, you may see several kinds of scores for each subject:

- *Raw Score*: This is simply the number of items your child got right and has no meaning by itself.

- *Grade Equivalent Score*: This tells what school grade your child's score matches for that subject. For example, a grade equivalent of 2.3 on Reading means that your child's reading skills are like those of most children in the third month of second grade.

- *Percentile Score*: This is a score from 1 to 100 that tells what percent of children scored lower than your child on each subtest. For example, a percentile score of 80 in spelling means that 79% of the children taking the test got a lower score than your child.

- *Stanine Score*: This is a general score from 1 (lowest) to 9 (highest). A score from 1-3 is below average, from 4-6 is average, and from 7-9 above average. This score can be used to compare your child's score with the general U.S. population.

Last, you will usually be able to compare your child's scores to both national and local norms. Local norms compare a child's score to others in your school district.

Generally, these tests give helpful information about what a child knows. However, if your child's scores were lower than you expected, consider (and help your child's teacher consider) these questions:
- What is your child's ability to read and write in English under timed conditions?
- Did your child understand the directions?
- Has your child ever taken tests like these before?
- Do your child's results indicate that s/he might benefit from additional support in certain areas?

Ask to meet with your child's teacher or guidance counselor if you have any questions or concerns about this testing.

## WHY DOESN'T MY CHILD HAVE TEXTBOOKS?

Decisions about what children will read are made by state or local school districts and individual teachers. Children in two different first-grade classes in the same school may not even have the same books. Many teachers feel they can put together an interesting and challenging set of readings that fit their children's interests and skills better than any single textbook. The use of primary sources (poetry, essays, historical documents, letters, etc.) is highly valued. Even in later grades when the use of textbooks may be more common, there are no nationally-used textbooks in the U.S.

## IF WE DON'T LIKE MY CHILD'S TEACHER, CAN WE ASK TO HAVE HER CHANGED TO ANOTHER TEACHER?

It is extremely rare for a child to change from one teacher to another in the middle of a school year. "Not liking" a teacher will rarely be seen by the school officials as an adequate reason for such a request. If, in high school, you feel strongly that a teacher in one subject is a very poor match for your child, it may be possible to switch to another section of the course, with a different teacher, halfway through the year, although this too is very rare. For the most part, your children will have to learn to work with the teachers to whom they are assigned. A guidance counselor or school psychologist may be able to help with any conflict that exists.

## THE TEACHER I OBSERVED DIDN'T SEEM TO BE DOING MUCH TEACHING. WHAT WAS GOING ON?

Generally speaking, the atmosphere in U.S. schools may seem

less academic than you expect, because of the American preference for active and integrated learning. Lecturing to a group of quiet, listening students, especially in elementary school, is rare. The classroom may seem less structured and more informal than in your country. Teaching periods devoted to academic subjects may be shorter than at home. And there may be a greater emphasis in the U.S. on interdisciplinary learning, with subjects being taught in an interrelated fashion. For example, the English and Social Studies teachers may work together to teach Shakespeare's play *Julius Caesar* during the history unit on ancient Rome. Teachers may use textbooks in a less methodical fashion, skipping around from chapter to chapter. This approach may strike you as less focused, but it may, instead, reflect a careful and creative lesson plan. If you are concerned about what your child is learning, ask to speak to the teacher.

## WHAT TRAINING DO THE TEACHERS HAVE?

The *No Child Left Behind Act* requires that teachers of core academic subjects at all levels of elementary and secondary education be qualified in their subject area(s) and in teaching. Some states also require teachers to continue their education over time. Certification programs are offered by universities and colleges as part of a four-year (bachelor's) undergraduate degree or as a graduate (post-bachelor's) program (often in combination with master's degree course work). To receive certification, prospective teachers must complete a series of education courses and a period of supervised practice teaching. See education. uky.edu/AcadServ/content/50-states-certification-requirements for links to teacher qualification standards in each state.

Private school teachers in most states do not need to be certified. It is up to the school to choose faculty with credentials that meet its needs and educational mission. Private secondary schools have historically been more interested in teachers with degrees in specific academic fields rather than a specialty in "education."

Although there are many gifted teachers in the U.S., teaching as a career path has not enjoyed the prestige or high pay in the United States that it has in some other parts of the world. This contributes to some unevenness in the quality of teachers and of teacher training programs.

### WILL MY CHILD PLAY SPORTS AT SCHOOL?

Students are generally required to attend a physical education class two or three times per week unless they have some medical problem or physical handicap. There will also probably be the opportunity to join after-school sports activities. These may range from informal supervised games among friends to highly competitive participation in regional *interscholastic* (between schools) sports associations. See Chapter 10 for more information on sports in high school

### WHAT ABOUT THE ARTS?

Many schools (from kindergarten through high school) offer a wide range of arts instruction and opportunities. Your child may be able — or even required — to study a musical instrument, be in a play, or take a drawing class. Many middle and high schools have optional bands, orchestras, drama clubs, dance groups, and art studios.

### WHAT OTHER KINDS OF ACTIVITIES BESIDES SPORTS AND ARTS WILL BE AVAILABLE?

In addition to athletic and arts programs, many schools sponsor debate teams, chess clubs, student publications, Girl and Boy

Scout groups, international exchange programs, and community-service opportunities (like helping at hospitals, animal shelters, or environmental agencies). Participation in these activities is usually voluntary, although community service is required in a number of school districts and in many private schools. Getting involved in some type of club or school-sponsored extracurricular group can be important to a child's successful adjustment to life in the U.S. Talk to the school administrative office, a guidance counselor, or your child's teachers to learn what types of activities are available. It is a good idea to get this information as soon as possible to ensure that your children can find space in the activities and groups that interest them.

#### WHY DOES THE TEACHER SEEM SO INTERESTED IN WHETHER MY CHILD HAS FRIENDS?

American educators tend to believe that children with solid friendships and good social skills are emotionally better prepared to learn. Besides providing the enjoyment that comes from being part of a social group, friends will also help your children practice English in a natural and spontaneous way.

#### WILL MY CHILD BE PREPARED TO RE-ENTER SCHOOL AT HOME AT THE END OF OUR STAY IN THE U.S.?

If your child will be returning to your home country's school system, it will be one of your most important jobs, as a parent, to give ongoing attention to necessary preparation for a return home. It will influence your choice of school, and your child's choice of subjects and course level. Explain to the school what your home educational system and demands are like, so they can help your child enroll in the best course of study.

You may find it helpful to enroll your children in supplementary educational programs (sometimes on weekends), to maintain their home language abilities and bolster the learning of some subjects. Maintaining the home language will be especially important for younger children, who may have learned to read and write while in the U.S. Practice in reading and writing their home language is sometimes best done in a formal supplementary educational program.

CHAPTER 9

# The Role of Parents, the Home, and Community

## WILL MY CHILD HAVE MUCH HOMEWORK?

It depends on your child's age. However, 95% of elementary-school children and 93% of high school students in the U.S. do some homework (an average of 1-1.5 hours/day). For young children, the purpose maybe simply to get them accustomed to the *process* of doing homework: remembering the assignment, bringing home the necessary papers or books, completing the assignment neatly, and remembering to bring it back to school. Homework assignments become more time consuming, difficult, and important as the child advances through school. Students who turn homework in late should expect to have points deducted from their grade. Final grades usually reflect performance on homework as well as on periodic tests, papers, classroom participation, and final examinations.

## HOW MUCH HOMEWORK HELP DO AMERICAN TEACHERS EXPECT PARENTS TO GIVE?

In the U.S., parents are expected to (a) be sure children do their homework but (b) not be *too* involved. American teachers want homework to teach more than just the school work. It should also teach independence, responsibility, and self-motivation. If parents are not active enough, the child may not learn the school work. But if parents are too active, the child may lose self-motivation. Getting that mix right is the family's job.

Some U.S. educators' recommendations about how to help a child with homework may sound too "American" to you. For example, one list from a group of American experts said you

## Parents Involvement with Children's Homework

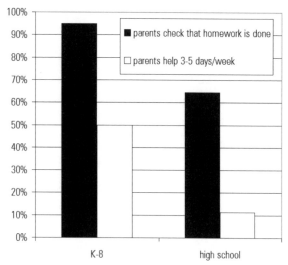

Source: National Center for Education Statistics

should give your children many choices, praise their ability, be non-directive, and ask about their feelings. Here's our list:

- **Give your child the necessary space.** Children differ in how much quiet they need, but most children do better if they have few distractions. A table, a comfortable chair, good light, and a quiet space are important.

- **Give your child the necessary tools.** This may simply mean a sharp pencil and a dictionary in English and your home language. Or a calculator and a library card. If your child's schoolwork requires a computer and you do not have one, the school will help you find a computer you can use.

- **Give your child the necessary time.** Help your child have enough time to finish homework by making clear family rules. You might say that homework must be finished before your child can play outside, talk on the telephone, watch TV or use the computer for recreation. You might limit the number of after-school activities your child joins.

- **Give your child the necessary help, but no more.** Children need to know what the assignments are, bring home the right books, plan enough time, know the right answers, write neatly, and finish their work. If your children can do all that alone, let them. If not, help them only with the part they cannot do. When you do help, do it in a way that teaches them how to work independently. For example, rather than simply looking to see if they finished the work, teach them to ask themselves, "How many problems was I supposed to do? How many did I do?"

- **Let your children know when you are pleased with their effort and work but be understanding when the work is difficult.** Americans tend to be direct in their praise of their children. You may have a different way, but you should do something to let your children know they have done well. Children generally work harder to earn approval than to avoid punishment.

- **Emphasize that working hard is effective.** One study in the U.S. showed that children of average ability who did three to five hours of homework per week got grades that were about the same as children of high ability who did no homework. Homework does make a difference. On the other hand, recognize that American parents around you may not emphasize effort as much as you might expect. Research has shown that American parents tend to attribute their children's school success and failure as being due, at least partly, to their native abilities rather than the amount of their effort. Getting the balance right between urging hard work and acknowledging real cognitive strengths and weaknesses will be important for you.

- **Talk to your child's teacher** if you think the homework is too easy or too hard, too much or too little. Tell the teacher your goals for your children. Explain the school system you have at home, especially if your child will be returning to it soon. Remember that you are in an American school where goals and methods are different. But try to develop a plan with the teacher that works for you both.

### AM I EXPECTED TO PARTICIPATE IN MY CHILD'S SCHOOL?

At the younger grades, yes. Many international newcomers are surprised at how involved American parents are with their children's elementary schools. Schools expect parents to:

- stop by the classroom to chat with the teacher periodically,
- observe or help in the classroom,
- volunteer time in the school library, student clubs, or special events,
- speak informally with the school principal from time to time,
- attend Parent-Teacher Organization (PTO) or Association (PTA) meetings,
- go with your child's class on trips to museums or plays,
- give money, items to sell, or time for fund-raising events.

Middle and high schools also welcome parental involvement in fund-raising, supervising school activities, and sharing their expertise and judgment. Schools at all levels expect parents to bring questions and concerns to them. Make an effort to meet your principal and guidance counselor, even if you do not have questions. Then, if you do, it will be easy to approach them for help.

## Home-School Involvement

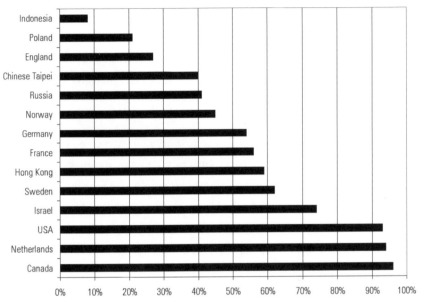

Note: Chart shows percent of principals who said that parents in their schools (a) are invited to parent-teacher conferences or well-attended parent events at least four times per year, (b) receive letters or newsletters about the school at least seven times per year, and (c) receive written reports of their children's academic progress at least four times per year.

Source: Progress in International Reading Literacy Study

### WHAT HAPPENS DURING A PARENT-TEACHER CONFERENCE?

It is common for elementary school teachers to meet individually with the parents of each child in the class once or twice each year. This meeting is *not* just for parents or children with problems or complaints. It is for everyone. It is a good time to review your child's education. If you think your child should have some extra services from the school (like more training in English, extra challenges in their strongest subjects, an assessment of special needs, extra help for their weakest subjects, or help in social areas), this is a good time to ask. If the conference is in the spring, you will be discussing plans for the fall. Teachers review each child's work and learning patterns and make recommendations for the kinds of teachers and courses the children should have.

You should be respectful of the school's professional judgment. Remember that the school staff must be concerned with the well-being of all the children in the school. But it is perfectly acceptable to make your ideas known.

Here are some practical tips, to help your conference go well:

- **It is best for both parents to go to the parent-teacher meeting, if possible.** Ask the teacher to try to schedule some meeting times that allow for parents' work schedules. (Some schools offer evening conference times for parents who cannot come during the day.) You will both have a better sense

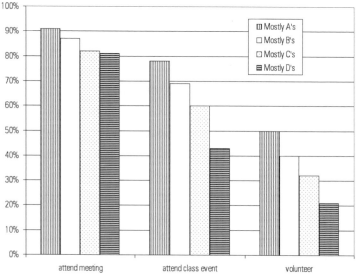

**Parental Involvement and Children's Grades in School**

- ▥ Mostly A's
- ☐ Mostly B's
- ☐ Mostly C's
- ▤ Mostly D's

Parents of children who got higher grades are more likely to have attended meetings and class events and to have volunteered at the school.

*Source: National Center for Education Statistics, National Household Education Survey*

of your child's school experience, and the teacher will appreciate your support and interest.

- **Be sure you understand all the teacher tells you.** It is easy for international *and* American parents to leave a school conference without really understanding the meaning of what the teacher has said. If the teacher talks about standardized test scores, ask what the tests measure, what the scores mean, and what the school does with the scores. If she talks about putting your child into a particular group based on academic level (such as a reading group or track) be sure you understand what this means. It is fine to ask the teacher to talk more slowly, and to repeat what she has said. Some international parents ask a friend whose English is very good to come to the conference with them.

- **Say something positive about the teacher and/or the school experience.** If you are pleased with how school is going, this will be easy, and Americans like an open expression of thanks. If you are unhappy with the school, saying something positive will help the teacher be more willing to listen to your criticism.

- **Ask for test records, work samples, reading lists, or curriculum descriptions**, if you think they will be helpful when you go back to your home country. Do this each year, even if you will not be returning home for some time. Your home school will appreciate having such clear information about what your child has studied.

## WHAT SHOULD I DO IF I HAVE A CONCERN OR WORRY ABOUT THE SCHOOL?

The differences between U.S. schools and those in your home country may surprise and worry you. They are surely a part of the cultural experience of living in this country. You may find that you welcome some of these differences. Others may conflict so much with your own cultural values that you cannot welcome them. In that case, your children will feel this conflict as well. It is important to work with the school to develop a way for your children not to feel caught between the two sets of values.

If you have concerns about something the teacher does, ask for a meeting with her before or after school, at a time you can be alone. Or ask her to call you on the telephone. Think ahead about how to discuss it. Have one or two specific examples in mind to discuss. Give the teacher time to explain her views. *Remember that you and the teacher are partners in your child's education.* Explain what schools are like in your own country, if it seems important. Make it clear that you understand this is an American school, but that you think it would be helpful if she understood your child's school history (and future, if you will be going home soon). Make specific suggestions if you can. ("My child tells me that when she is slow in doing her work, she gets very worried. Did you know she sometimes comes home and cries? I find that giving her a 5-minute-warning that the time is almost over is very helpful at home.") Then, wait a week or two to see if the situation improves. If it does not, it is fine to talk to someone else in the school about your concern. You might try the guidance counselor, the principal, or the headmaster. But start with the teacher.

If you have concerns about something else (like a relationship with another child or with a school policy), the teacher is usually the best place to start. Ask for a meeting or for a telephone call.

If these steps do not solve the problem, go to the person at the school you feel most comfortable with and ask for help in how to proceed. This might be a guidance counselor or ESL teacher, the school secretary or another teacher. If the problem involves other children, describe the problem in general terms without giving names, to protect the other children's privacy. Ask for help in how to proceed.

### HOW CAN I BE SURE MY CHILD GETS THE BEST TEACHER?

You probably cannot "be sure" that your child will be assigned to any particular teacher. Many schools have a policy that parents cannot make requests for specific teachers — some teachers would get too many requests and others not enough. However:

- Realize that rumors about teachers' reputations are not always right. A teacher who is "not good" for one child (or parent!) may be "wonderful" for another.

- You may be able to talk with (or write to) the principal describing the *type* of teacher you want your child to have. Say you think your child will learn better with a teacher who is "nurturing and kind, rather than too strict" (for example). Describe the traits of the teacher you want. But do not criticize the other teacher(s). The principal may be more open to this kind of request than a request for one specific teacher.

### WHAT CAN I DO TO HELP MY CHILD AS THE "NEW KID" AT SCHOOL?

Some children and teenagers love the chance to be the "new kid." They like feeling special. And they like the fact that no one knew them when they had that awful short haircut, before they learned to read, or when they were overweight! Other children find the transition to a new school to be difficult.

In several ways, moving to a new school in the U.S. may be easier than moving to other countries. First, about 17% of school-age children move to a different home each year, usually in the summer. So your children will probably not be the only "new kids" in your school.

Second, in most elementary schools, all children start in new class groups each September. They will be with a new teacher and many children they do not know. From seventh to twelfth grades, most children move from class to class (and teacher to teacher) for different subjects. So "new kids" may not be very obvious.

Of course, these same reasons can mean that your child may feel lost and ignored rather than special. Here are some ideas to help your children be the "new kid:"

- **If you arrive in the U.S. during the summer, visit the school a day or two before the first day of class.** Most schools will let you walk around and find the toilets, the lunchroom, the gym, the office, the ESL room, the library, and any other place they might be asked to walk without a teacher. Ask the principal if you and your children could see the room they will be in. If the teacher is there, it will be a nice, quiet moment to meet. Spend a few minutes sitting in the room and looking around. Your children will feel more comfortable when classes begin and the first day won't feel as scary.

- **Spend some time in the school playground.** In the summer, playgrounds are open to the public and many children gather there to play. Even if your children do not "make friends," they will start to understand how American children play. And the other children will begin to recognize them.

- **Be proud of your children**, even if their adjustment seems slow to you. Children are accomplishing many major tasks in the early days. Their English is new. The goals and methods of the school are different from what they have mastered at home. They know no one except their siblings. And yet they soon learn, make friends, and play alongside the others. Children are resilient, flexible, and creative. They will use these skills more easily if they feel your support and pride.

- **Do not hurry your children academically.** Learning occurs more easily when children feel comfortable and stable. In the early days of your life in the U.S., it may be more important for your children to make friends and learn about the school than it is to get top grades. Remember that learning to master a new culture, a new language, new friendship patterns, and a new educational system *is* a kind of learning. These may be more important life lessons than the math, science or history facts in the classroom.

- **Help your children make friends.** This is not simply so that your children will have more fun. Research in the U.S. shows that children who have problems with friends are more likely to have problems with school learning, problems with adults, and problems later in life. Children do not need *lots* of friends — some like big groups, some like having just one close friend. What is important is that they learn to share, cooperate, be kind, and feel accepted.

**HERE ARE SOME IDEAS TO HELP YOUR CHILD MAKE FRIENDS:**

- For younger children, *spend time after school hours in the playground.* Informal play time, and simply being seen and becoming familiar, will help.

- Have your child join some *after-school activity*, like a sports team, chess team, or art club. Friendships may grow more easily here than during school.

- Ask the school office if there are any *other international families*, including any from your country, who are currently at the school. Contacts like these may help you set up a network of support and friendships, because you will share similar experiences.

- *Invite other children to your home* after school or on weekends, or to a game, museum, or movie.

- *Invite a whole family* to your house, or to do an activity together. Sometimes, young children are more comfortable playing with new children if their families are there.

- Try to *find ways to do your children's favorite activities.* Teenagers, especially, miss being in situations where they excel. Try to find activities that are similar to their favorite ones at home. For example, find one that requires team cooperation (even if the sport is different) or artistic ability (even if the art or craft is different).

## WHAT COMMUNITY RESOURCES ARE AVAILABLE TO HELP MY CHILD AND ME?

Each community in the U.S. has many resources that can be useful to you in solving particular problems and in introducing you and your children to new friends:

- **public libraries:** any resident in that community can borrow books for free (bring proof of residence the first time you go — like a local drivers' license, a utilities bill, or a lease); most public libraries have computers with Internet access; resource books on buying cars or finding jobs; books and videotapes in foreign languages and ESL materials; classes for adults; story hours for children; film series, etc.;

- **religious organizations:** in the U.S., churches, synagogues, mosques, and other religious organizations are not only places for worship, but are also centers for sharing activities with people with similar values;

- **community mental health centers:** the job of these centers is to provide for the well-being of all community residents, and to prevent problems from developing; psychotherapy is offered, often at reduced fees for those who need it; other services are offered through schools and social service agencies;

- **recreation departments:** your community may have a recreation center with a pool, tennis and/or basketball courts, fitness machines, and classes for adults and children; some may offer sports teams as well, as an alternative o the school-based ones;

- **emergency services:** look in the front of your White Pages telephone book for a list of telephone numbers of agencies that can help in medical, psychological, child-rearing, or housing emergencies;

- **activity programs:** your community may have Boy or Girl Scout groups, art programs, and other programs that offer the opportunity to meet children in supervised ways.

CHAPTER 10
# High School Issues


## WHAT ARE THE GRADUATION REQUIREMENTS IN THE U.S.?

There are no national graduation requirements for what courses or exams a student must pass. Each state or school district sets its minimum requirements. However, many states follow at least some of the recommendations of a National Commission on Excellence in Education: four years of English; three years each of mathematics, science and social studies; one semester of computer science; and, for college-bound students, two years of a foreign language. Many require at least one year of American History and some amount of physical education.

Each high school has its own system to manage whether a student has met graduation requirements. This is typically done

---

### QUESTIONS TO ASK WHEN YOU VISIT A HIGH SCHOOL

- *"How will you determine my children's academic achievement level in order to give them proper credit for their previous study in a subject area? How will their previous study be applied to your graduation requirements?"*

- *"I am looking for a challenging program for my children. How will you determine what classes they should take?"*

- *"How do I know if my children are prepared and qualified to take Advanced Placement (AP) courses?"*

- *"How do I know if my child is prepared and qualified to take the International Baccalaureate program? What courses would be required of them? How difficult are the courses and the examinations? When do students decide whether to try for the IB diploma versus choosing to earn IB certificates in individual subjects?"*

- *"In addition to the state and local requirements, does your school have any other graduation requirements (like community service, driver's education, health, state history, or state exams) that will apply to my children?"*

---

through the tracking of "credits." Some schools assign one credit for each year-long course that meets one 40-minute period per day. Others use a credit system that reflects the number of sessions a class meets per week. For example, a class that meets five days per week would earn five credits; a class that meets three days would earn three credits. Be sure to get a list of your child's school's graduation requirements.

**THE STATE WE HAVE MOVED TO REQUIRES HIGH SCHOOL STUDENTS TO PASS A STATE-WIDE TEST IN ORDER TO GRADUATE; WILL THIS TEST APPLY TO US?**

About half the states in the U.S. require public school students to pass an exit exam in order to graduate from high school. (Only nine states require private school students to do so.) Most of these require 10th grade proficiency (or higher) in English/language arts and mathematics. Over the next few years, many states plan to add exams in science and history to their requirements. Be sure to find out what rules apply in your state for students from other countries, especially if you will be moving into the state near your child's time of graduation.

**WHAT SHOULD I DO TO BE SURE MY HIGH SCHOOL CHILD WILL BE ABLE TO GRADUATE ON TIME?**

Requirements for graduation vary among schools and depend upon the number of years a student spends in an American secondary school before graduation. If your child is 16, 17 or 18 years old when you move and is entering the 11th or 12th grade, be sure that s/he selects courses that will allow for graduation. Some courses have *prerequisites* (courses that must be taken beforehand). Other courses last two or more terms. Review the high school's course catalogue and handbook for this kind of information. Planning ahead can maximize flexibility.

To ensure that your children's school understands their prior education, you might consider having their transcripts translated and evaluated by an independent service (see Chapter 5 for information about such services).

Some international students have had unfortunate misunderstandings about high school graduation requirements. When you enroll your child into a high school, ask for a careful examination of your child's selection of courses to be sure that s/he is on course to graduate on time with the rest of the class. It is a good idea to ask for this confirmation in writing so there are no complications at the end of the senior year.

### WHAT IS A GUIDANCE COUNSELOR?

Your high school student will be assigned to a guidance counselor (sometimes called a school counselor) who can help with academic questions, planning for the future, or general growth and development issues. Parents may also meet with the guidance counselor, if you like.

## Goals Emphasized by Guidance Counselors

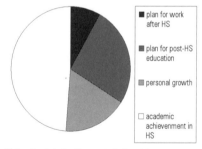

- plan for work after HS
- plan for post-HS education
- personal growth
- academic achievenment in HS

*Percent of public high schools indicating goals their guidance programs emphasized most;*
*Source: The Condition of Education*

### WHAT IS THE "G.E.D.?"

The General Educational Development (G.E.D.) Testing Service offers a high-school equivalency certificate to those who pass its national test. The test involves essay writing and testing of knowledge in math, social studies, science, and interpreting literature and the arts. To pass the test, applicants must perform as well as or better than 67% of a sample of that year's high school graduating seniors. To take the G.E.D. test, applicants must be at least 16-18 years old (depending on which state they live in), not be enrolled in high school, and not be a high school graduate. Each state may set additional rules about age, residency in the state, and length of time since leaving school. About 98% of U.S. colleges and universities accept the G.E.D. diploma instead of a high school diploma. The average person taking the G.E.D. test is about 25 years old and left high school at about the 10th grade. Typically, applicants have taken the G.E.D. to gain entrance to college, to get a job that requires a high school education, or for a general sense of accomplishment.

### WHAT ARE "AP COURSES?"

"AP" (Advanced Placement) courses are taught at a more advanced level than standard courses. The majority of U.S. high schools offer at least one AP course. High schools may offer them in a number of subjects, and students may choose which subjects, if any, they would like to take at the AP level. The most common AP offerings are in English literature, U.S. History, and Calculus, but your school may also offer AP courses in such topics as biology, chemistry, English and other languages, European history, U.S. government, art history, statistics and economics. About one-third of public high schools offer AP courses in the four core subject areas, and about one-fourth of U.S. students take an AP course in their high school career.

After completing an AP course, students may take a national AP exam in that subject. Students who get a score of 3, 4, or 5 on the exam may be able to skip the first level university course or earn university credit for that course. If your child will attend university outside the U.S., scores on an AP exam may be used in the admissions process as an indicator of academic achievement. For more information, go to apcentral.collegeboard.com.

In recent years, educators have been debating the strengths and weaknesses of the AP program. Many have expressed concern that the AP exam has dictated excessively the content and pace of the classes they teach. Consequently, many fine private schools have recently dropped official AP courses, providing comparable Honors courses instead. The College Board is in the process of revising its curriculum for AP courses.

### WHAT ABOUT IB COURSES?

Please see a description of International Baccalaureate courses in Chapter 2. Only 2% of U.S. public high schools offer IB courses.

### WHAT ARE "DUAL CREDIT" COURSES?

Dual credit courses are high school courses but are considered college-level, and therefore earn students both high school and post-secondary credits. Typically, they exist through a partnership between a high school and another institution such as a local college. 71% of public U.S. high schools offer at least one dual credit course.

### MY CHILD IS VERY INTERESTED IN SPORTS. WHAT CAN WE EXPECT AT A U.S. HIGH SCHOOL?

The most common high school sports are swimming, basketball, and American football, but, depending on the location and resources of the school, they may also have teams in gymnastics, lacrosse, field and ice hockey, tennis, volleyball, soccer (football), skiing, sailing, and more. Students of varying athletic abilities may be able to participate. Competition and team work are important for forming friendships. You may be surprised at the level of enthusiasm that surrounds high school sports. Students may be expected to show "school spirit" in support of their teams, and high school athletes may enjoy high status among their peers.

Interscholastic athletic programs often require a great deal of time and commitment and may involve substantial additional expense. Athletes who compete in a school's interscholastic sports program may be exempt from the school's physical education courses.

Students who are especially talented in athletics may want to continue their sport at a competitive level once attending a U.S. university. Preparation for this must begin in high school. In the United States there is a governing body for university level athletics (the National Collegiate Athletic Association, or NCAA). There are three divisions or levels of university play — Division I, II and III. If your children are interested in playing on a Division I or II team, they must comply with the processes in place by the NCAA. There are rules about students talking with coaches, about coaches planning student visits to the university to meet the team, about tryouts, and most importantly, about academic and testing requirements. The guidance office at your child's school can give you more information Or visit www.ncaa.org.

**WHAT SHOULD WE BE DOING ABOUT UNIVERSITY ADMISSION?**
The university application process is beyond the scope of this book — if your child will be attending college or university in the U.S., be sure to work closely with the high school guidance

department to learn about deadlines for testing and applications, and to get a sense about how to choose the right colleges for your child. To learn about different colleges' application requirements and characteristics, look at the college's website. Or go to a public library, book store, or your high school office for books that discuss this information. You should also visit www.collegeboard.com, which is where you can register on-line to take the SAT. That site also has a college search function and information on financial aid.

If your child will be attending university in your home country, try to talk with a representative of your home country's university *before* your child starts high school in the U.S. An International Baccalaureate (IB) degree will probably be the most meaningful record, but Advanced Placement (AP) courses and high SAT scores may also be accepted by universities in other countries. On the other hand, it may be that high marks in non-AP courses at a U.S. high school along with a high school diploma may qualify your child for entrance to these universities.

# The Education Passport

All mobile families should maintain an Education Passport for each of their school-age children. While requirements vary, schools often request the materials listed below. The Education Passport will also assist students when they apply to college. The list of items below is comprehensive; not all of the suggested documentation may be necessary or obtainable for a given child. Well-documented education files will greatly facilitate placement procedures.

☐ Names and addresses of schools attended and dates of attendance.

☐ Transcripts: copies of course lists, grades, and evaluations, translated into English if necessary.

☐ Description of the home curriculum: both an official version and teachers' outlines of the program are useful, as are copies of the most recent Math and English textbooks.

☐ Standardized testing results and evaluations.

☐ Examples of your child's work: completed assignments from the most recent academic period, writing samples or special projects.

☐ Medical records: an immunization history; information on specific conditions that might affect the child's participation in any part of a school program.

☐ Results of a full recent physical examination conducted by a doctor in the U.S. if possible.

☐ Birth certificate and/or, for non-U.S. citizens, a passport and visa.

☐ Public schools require proof of residency — usually a lease or electric, sewer, or water bill addressed to you at your home.

☐ Any standardized testing that may help explain a child's special abilities or needs.

# Index

educational consultant, 41
elective courses, 75
elementary school, 35-37, 73-74
emergency services in community, 107
English as a second language, 48-49, 78-82
   tips for helping children, 81-83
enrichment programs, see "ability-based teaching"
enrollment, see "registration"
excused absence note, 65
extracurricular activities, 10, 92-93

field trip, 65
financial aid, 28
foreign language, teaching of, 74-75
friends, importance of for learning, 48-49, 92
   tips for making, 103-106
funding, school, 17-20, 41

General Educational Development (G.E.D.) Testing Service, 111-112
geography, see "social studies, teaching of"
gifted and talented programs, see "ability-based teaching"
grades, see "report cards"
graduate student, 8
graduation requirements, 109-111
guidance counselor, 46, 83-85, 111

headmaster, see "principal"
high school, 31, 35-39, 75, 109-115
   diploma, 29, 31, 35, 109-111
history, see "social studies, teaching of"
holidays, see "vacations"
homeroom, 65
homework, 95-98
   parental help, 97
   tips for helping with, 95-98
Honor Roll, 86
honors courses, see "ability-based teaching"

I.E.P. see "Individualized Education Program"
illness and school absence, 70-71
immunizations required, 53-54
independent school, 23 (also see "private school")
individualism, 11-12, 87
Individualized Education Program, 84-85

single-sex education, 33
social development, see "friends"
social studies, teaching of, 74-75
special needs, 83-85
specialization, educational, 9
spelling, teaching of, 11, 73-74, 77
sports, 92, 113-114 (also see "physical education")
    NCAA, 114
S.S.A.T:, see "Secondary School Admission Test"
standardized tests, 87-90
    meaning of scores, 88-90
student expenditure, 19, 44
teachers, 44-45, 90-92
    salaries, 44-45
    selecting, 90
    training of, 91-92
teaching methods, 76-78, 90-91
textbooks, use of, 90
tracking, see "ability-based teaching"
transcript translation, 57, 111
transportation to and from school, 67-68
typing, see "keyboarding"

undergraduate, 8
uniforms, 69
university, 6-10, 114
    admission, 114-115
    graduate student, 8
    international comparison of completion rates, 7
    liberal arts, 6-8
    proportion high school graduates attending, 6, 7, 43
    undergraduate, 8
    vs. college, 8
upper school, see "high school"
urban vs. suburban schools, 21-22, 49-50

vacations, 63-66
values, educational, 10-14, 46-49
visiting schools, 45-50
vouchers, 23, 24, 31

# Additional Resources for International Newcomers

Please visit **The Interchange Institute**'s web site (www.interchangeinstitute.org) to order additional copies of this book and other useful materials for newcomers to the United States, including:

*Newcomer's Almanac* and *English Practice Worksheet*
A unique collection of information, advice, and cultural interpretation for international newcomers to the United States in a 12-page monthly newsletter. Targeted to meet the needs of individuals and families on temporary assignment or who have recently immigrated, *Newcomer's Almanac* is a transitional lifeline of practical tips and thoughtful analysis of American culture.

*Hello! USA* (by Judy Priven and Anne P. Copeland), 5th edition
A book filled with practical facts and tips about how to move to the U.S. from another country. Visas, Social Security numbers, credit cards, utilities, computers, job hunting, and much more.

*Welcome Files*
A set of 13 laminated cards and pamphlets with practical information newcomers to the United States need when they first arrive.

*Global Baby: Tips to Keep You and Your Infant Smiling Before, During, and After Your International Move* (by Anne P. Copeland, Ph.D.)
A short, practical guide to help you make an international move with an infant.

*A Smooth Beginning: 20 Suggestions to Help Your Family Feel Settled in a New Country*
A short workbook and list of tips.

### The Interchange Institute
www.interchangeinstitute.org
Telephone: (617) 566 2227
Email: orders@interchangeinstitute.org
Fax: (617) 277 0889

The website of **Bennett Schoolplacement Worldwide** (www.schoolplacement.com) includes information on educational consulting services for families and corporations as well as articles of interest to families relocating with school-aged children. There, you can also order:

*The Guide to International Education in the United States: National Curriculum and International Schools*

Lists contact and descriptive information for all international and I.B. schools, and British, French, German, Italian, Japanese, and Spanish national curriculum schools in the U.S. Lists schools by nationality and location, names of directors, grade levels and school day format, date established and current enrollment numbers, and accreditation granting organization.

### Bennett Schoolplacement Worldwide
www.schoolplacement.com
Telephone: (215) 554-1656